Microprocessor 2

Series Editor
Jean-Charles Pomerol

Microprocessor 2

Core Concepts –
Communication in a Digital System

Philippe Darche

iSTE

WILEY

Quotation

Every advantage has its disadvantages and vice versa.

Shadokian philosophy[1]

1 The Shadoks are the main characters from an experimental cartoon produced by the Research Office of the Office de Radiodiffusion-Télévision Française (ORTF). The two-minute-long episodes of this daily cult series were broadcast on ORTF's first channel (the only one at the time!) beginning in 1968. The birds were drawn simply and quickly using an experimental device called an *animograph*.

The Shadoks are ridiculous, stupid and mean. Their intellectual capacities are completely unusual. For example, they are known for bouncing up and down, but it is not clear why! Their vocabulary consists of four words: GA, BU, ZO and MEU, which are also the four digits in their number system (base 4) and the musical notes in their four-tone scale. Their philosophy is comprised of famous mottos such as the one cited in this book.

The second volume is devoted to aspects of communication in digital systems from the point of view of buses. Their main characteristics are presented, as well as their communication, access arbitration, and transaction protocols, their interfaces and their electrical characteristics. A classification is proposed and the main buses are described.

The third volume deals with the hardware aspects of the microprocessor. It first details the component's external interface and then its internal organization. It then presents the various commercial generations and certain specific families such as the Digital Signal Processor (DSP) and the microcontroller. The volume ends with a presentation of the datasheet.

The fourth volume deals with the software aspects of this component. The main characteristics of the Instruction Set Architecture (ISA) of a generic component are detailed. We then study the two ways to alter the execution flow with both classic and interrupt function call mechanisms.

The final volume presents the hardware and software aspects of the development chain for a digital system as well as the architectures of the first microcomputers in the historical perspective.

Multi-level organization

This book gradually transitions from conceptual to physical implementation. Pedagogy was my main concern, without neglecting formal aspects. Reading can take place on several levels. Each reader will be presented with introductory information before being asked to understand more difficult topics. Knowledge, with a few exceptions, has been presented linearly and as comprehensively as possible. Concrete examples drawn from former and current technologies illustrate the theoretical concepts.

When necessary, exercises complete the learning process by examining certain mechanisms in more depth. Each volume ends with bibliographic references including research articles, works and patents at the origin of the concepts and more recent ones reflecting the state of the art. These references allow the reader to find additional and more theoretical information. There is also a list of acronyms used and an index covering the entire work.

This series of books on computer architecture is the fruit of over 30 years of travels in the electronic, microelectronic and computer worlds. I hope that it will provide you with sufficient knowledge, both practical and theoretical, to then specialize in one of these fields. I wish you a pleasant stroll through these different worlds.

IMPORTANT NOTES. – As this book presents an introduction to the field of microprocessors, references to components from all periods are cited, as well as references to computers from generations before this component appeared.

Original company names have been used, although some have merged. This will allow readers to find specification sheets and original documentation for the mentioned integrated circuits on the Internet and to study them in relation to this work.

The concepts presented are based on the concepts studied in selected earlier works (Darche 2000, 2002, 2003, 2004, 2012), which I recommend reading beforehand.

Philippe DARCHE
July 2020

Introduction

This volume consists of four chapters and looks at the microprocessor and its communication system, linking its different components, or functional subunits, both internally and externally. Communication revolves around the notion of the "bus". The bus is the backbone of all communication, and forms a "digital information highway". It has been, and remains, the preferred form of interconnection in computer systems. However, just like on a highway, this shared communication medium is also one of (von Neumann) bottlenecks, which arise when all of the connected entities want to use it at the same time. Astute design and sizing are therefore vital for maximizing computer performance. Here, we present their main characteristics, the protocols for communication, access arbitration and transaction, their interfacing, and the electric aspects. Some of these points have already been covered, notably with regard to the memory channel (Darche 2012), but here, they are completed and generalized. A system of classification is then suggested. The topic is closed with On-Chip Communication (OCC) and multiprocessor aspects.

1

Basic Definitions

In order to describe communication between components and electronic subunits, first we must cover general notions such as the direction of communication and connection topology, as well as the concepts of exchange synchronization and information coding, finishing off with the concept of a protocol, which defines the rules that have to be followed. A protocol also defines access arbitration and cycles.

1.1. General points regarding communication

The direction of communication between two systems (Figure 1.1) can either be one-way (simplex) or bidirectional, and this can be either a full-duplex or alternating (half-duplex). Note here that the communication protocol (i.e. the link layer) cannot provide more than what the physical layer permits.

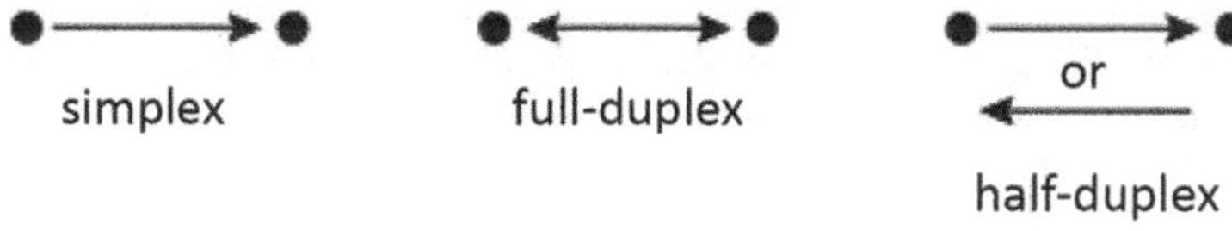

Figure 1.1. *Direction of transmission*

The entity from which the communication originates and which is generating the address and control signals is called the Master (M) or Initiator (I), and is represented by a square in Figure 1.2. The entity that replies and follows the commands is traditionally called the Slave (S), or Target (T), and this is represented by a square in the figure. If the bus can only take a single master, it is referred to as a single master system. If it can take several it is called a multi-master system (*cf.* § 2.2.5). If the medium is shared during emission, there can be a conflict of access to the resource (i.e. the bus or slave unit); this is called a collision. The collision can be either logical or physical. A physical collision can result in material damage if the electronic output stage is not designed for it. For this reason, access arbitration is needed (*cf.* § 1.6).

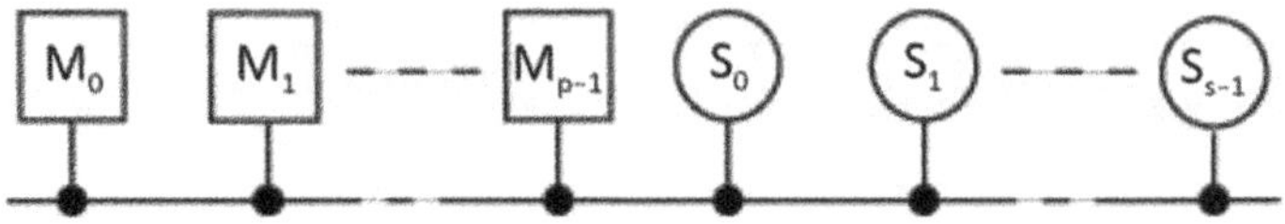

Figure 1.2. *Model of a multi-master bus*

To access the bus, each entity requires an interface called I/F (Figure 1.3).

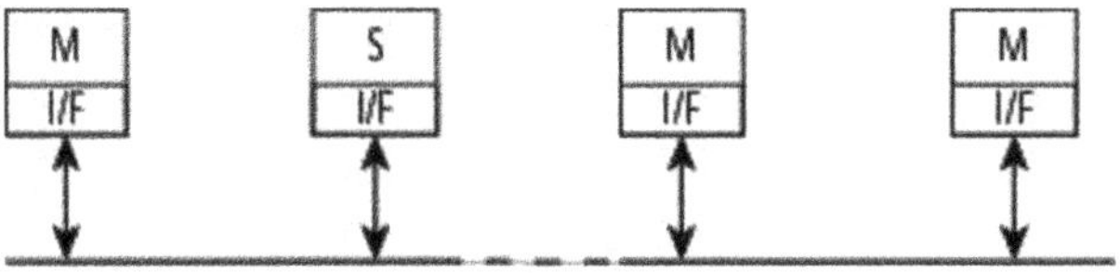

Figure 1.3. *Shared bus*

In a one-way bus (simplex transmission), an emitter Tx can emit towards one or several receivers Rx. This is a *divergent* bus, which can broadcast information (Figure 3.16, for example, and *cf.* § 2.2). Another case that must be considered is where several emitters can only communicate towards a single receiver. This is a *convergent* bus that allows for the broadcall of information (*cf.* § 2.2). The existence of several masters can result in an issue of *contention* when multiple access requests are made to the communication carrier. The bus can be bidirectional (Figure 3.14, for example), with simultaneous transmission (full-duplex), or alternating transmission (half-duplex).

There are several topological variations, including the MUX-based bus (multiplex) and the AND–OR structure. Both are preferred to the SoC (System on (a) Chip). They are shown in Figure 4.28(a) and (b) respectively.

Since there are three main types of information (address, data and control) to be passed around the nodes of a bus in a microprocessor system, there are several ways for them to be transported: there are three combinations with one element, three combinations with two and one with three possibilities. These combinations specialize the bus, resulting in address buses, data buses, control buses, address–

control buses, address–data buses, control–data buses and address–control–data buses (only one bus!). During an exchange of several types of information between two entities, for example, between an address and a piece of data, the transfer can make use of separate media (non-multiplexed bus), or they can use the same medium (multiplexed bus). The choice to multiplex is often one of cost: a bus takes up physical space on the Printed Circuit Board (PCB), which is expensive. The number of output connection points for each electronic component and even for the connectors must be taken into account, as the cost of an Integrated Circuit (IC) or a connector is directly linked to this amount. The first approach is better in terms of bitrate, as the buses are separate, with one for each information type. Time-division multiplexing[1] is a solution that allows several different types of information to travel through the same bus, but at different times. The initial philosophy at Intel was that of multiplexing the address and data buses. An example is the 8088 microprocessor made by Intel for the IBM PC (Personal Computer, *cf.* § V5-3.2.1). This was in contrast to Motorola, which did not multiplex its address and data buses. Another example is the PCI (Peripheral Component Interconnect, *cf.* § 4.2.4). It should be noted that the information required for the transaction does not need to be presented all at the same time. For example, the information to be written can be presented after the address ("late write", *cf.* § 4.4.1 in Darche (2012)). The flipside of multiplexing is that the information transfer time is usually longer as the information has to be (de)multiplexed before it can be accessed, resulting in delays in propagation. This can be done either through a process that is external to the communicating elements, or internally, and thus transparently. In the former option, the peripheral circuits communicate specifically with a microprocessor, usually belonging to the same commercial family, for example, the MPU (MicroProcessor Unit, µP for short) 8085 from Intel and its parallel interface circuit 8155, where the former's (de)multiplexers were integrated into the latter. In the case of a bus with different pieces of information spread over different moments in time, multiplexing does not slow down the exchanges and therefore cannot reduce the bitrate.

1.2. Main characteristics

A shared bus is a common interconnection pathway between all of the connected nodes. It is made of a set of lines or communication channels along which the information flows. Usually, only signals are counted, as the power and grounding lines are contained in a separate power bus (*cf.* § 4.2.10). This number does not take into account electrical characteristics, for example, whether the signal is differential or not (*cf.* § 3.6.3 in Darche (2012)). At least three[2] elements or nodes can connect to

1 Frequency-Division Multiplexing (FDM) is not suitable here.

2 Some authors, Borrill (1981), for example, consider a bus to be formed of the connection of two or more elements.

it; otherwise, it would be a point-to-point connection, also known as a link. These elements can be electronic components, electronic boards, peripherals or computer systems, depending on the level of observation. These buses can also be inside computer systems, particularly in a microprocessor (*cf.* § 4.2.9). Information is considered in a broad sense in this work, so it can refer to data, an address[3], a command, a control, a state or even an interrupt request or its vector (*cf.* § V4-5.7). These lines are usually permanently grouped by information type or by function. The result is referred to as a dedicated bus. Two examples are the address bus and the memory channel (*cf.* § 7.2 in Darche (2012)). Thurber *et al.* (1972) define these buses as functionally dedicated[4]. A dedicated bus is more expensive in terms of connectors and electronics, but its interface is simpler in terms of design (no (de)multiplexing, for example). Otherwise it is undedicated. As the technology used is electric or electronic, the bus takes the form of electric conductors (electric ribbon cables, metallic traces in a printed or integrated circuit) through which the electric signals travel, most of the time in two states. Optics is a possible future development, but it remains currently under research (*cf.*, for example, Feldman *et al.* (1999)). Fiber optics are used extensively throughout networks, however.

A bus can be of a unique design, produced by computer or microprocessor makers, or a regulated solution that follows established standards, coming from private solutions, or not. A standardized solution, which by definition provides generic characteristics, is usually less effective than an *ad hoc* solution, but it is usually cheaper due to the standardization of its components and systems (Commercial Off-The-Shelf (COTS) solution). In particular, defining a standard for the interface helps with design as it allows for interoperability and reuse of the modules.

A bus is characterized mainly by its width w (w bit-wide), its bitrate (incorrectly referred to as its transfer speed) and by its communication protocol that defines its signals. The typical values of w are 1, 4, 8 and multiples thereof, usually of eight. This is particularly true for data buses, as the data that passes through them are themselves multiples of eight[5]. The address bus, however, can also be expressed in other multiples, for example, the 8086 microprocessor from Intel whose address bus

3 An address is a digital label that takes the form of an integer, and is linked to a location or memory cell.

4 He adds to the definition that a bus can only be physically dedicated if a pair of elements belong to the bus and use it exclusively. We shall not keep this addition as this would be a link according to our own definition.

5 A counter-example is the 12-bit data format in the PDP-8/E mini-computer from Digital Equipment Corporation (DEC).

has a width of 20 bits. The width of the address bus gives the addressing capacity $C = 2^w$ memory words of the component that generated the address, which is usually the microprocessor. It therefore defines its Address Space (AS, *cf.* § V3-2.1.1.1). It represents the amount of physical memory accessible without any additional mechanisms, such as Virtual Memory (VM, *cf.* V2 on semiconductor memory). The width of address buses and data buses do not have to correlate with each other. Some examples are: (m/n) 16/8 (8-bit generation microprocessor), 16/16 and 21/16 (first-generation 16-bit microprocessor), 24/32 and 32/32 (32-bit generation microprocessor), etc. The width of the data bus is linked to the flow of information (*cf.* below).

A serial bus has a single communication channel ($w = 1$). A parallel bus has w channels ($w > 1$). In the first case, this means that only a single bit is sent at a time. In order to send a piece of data in the format n > 1, serialization must first take place, with the inverse operation, deserialization, taking place upon reception of the data (Figure 1.4). The number of signals is therefore low, which reduces the connection cost (cables, surface area and therefore number of PCB traces, connectors[6] and number of IC package pins). There is no time delay between signals from different lines. Moreover, scalability, that is, increasing the bitrate, is made easier as all that is required is to increase the number of links. Serial communication is used in linked connections, mainly in Input/Output (I/O) interfaces. It can also be used in a bus, for example, in the coaxial cable Ethernet network IEEE 802.3™-2008 10Base2 and 10Base5 (IEEE 2008). There is a disadvantage in terms of bandwidth as service bits must be used in order to synchronize the exchange (start and stop bits of the interface RS-232 (RS for Recommended Standard), for example, *cf.* § 8.2.2 in Darche (2003)) and to detect and possibly correct transmission errors. Moreover, (de)serialization takes time. Each communicating element has a (de)serializer that either includes or rebuilds the clock signal, depending on the case. This is the SerDes (Serializer/Deserializer) technology. The SPMT™ (Serial Port Memory Technology) uses this technology (*cf.* § 3.6.8 in Darche (2012)). SerDes type transfers usually utilize an 8b/10b encoding (Widmer and Franaszek 1983), which is 8 bits of information encoded into 10 bits in order to eliminate the Direct Current (DC) of the signal (DC-balanced) so that the clock signal can be rebuilt. The useful bitrate is then equal to 80% of the raw bitrate.

6 This statement is true, but it is important to remember the counter-example of the RS-232 link (EIA 1991 1997), which uses a 25-pin D-Sub connector with only eight effective signals and the ground (*cf.* § 8.2.2 in Darche (2003)).

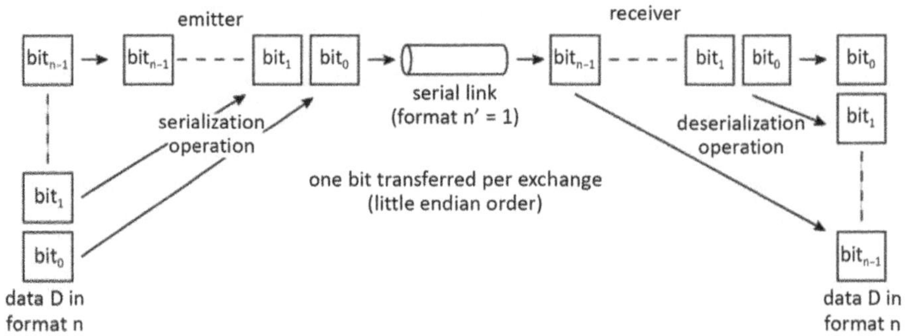

Figure 1.4. *(De)serialization operations in the serial link*

In parallel transmission, n (n > 1) bits are sent to an exchange when the format of the data n is equal to that of the interface (Figure 1.5). The word to be transmitted can have a higher format, for example k × n bits, $k \in \mathbb{N}^*$. Parallel transmission will then take place in subwords of n bits. In this case, it is called subword-parallel transmission.

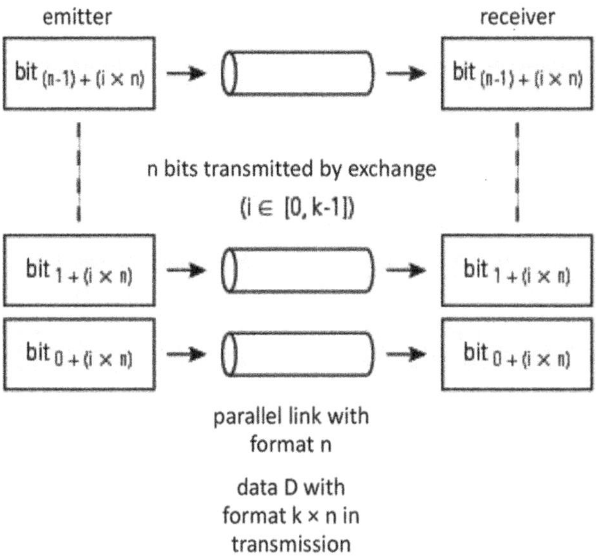

Figure 1.5. *Format n parallel link*

In that last case and in the case of serial transmission, there is the issue of the order in which bits and bytes are sent. This is the problem of Little Endian (LE) and Big Endian (BE), identified by Cohen (1981) (*cf.* § 2.6.2 in Darche (2012) and § V1-2.2.1). James (1990) explored this problem looking at the bus specifically. Note that the byte swapping function, as present either as a microprocessor instructions (`bswap`, for example, *cf.* § V4-2.6.1), or implemented in bus interface circuits (a bridge, for example) or in communication circuits or controllers (*cf.* Sriti (1999), for example) allows for this order to be reversed. Moreover, for the last mode, there can be an issue with the alignment (*cf.* § 2.6.1 in Darche (2012)), meaning that a word in the format n is not transmitted in a single bus cycle, but rather over two cycles, as shown in the examples of Figure 1.6 for a transmission in the 32-bit format.

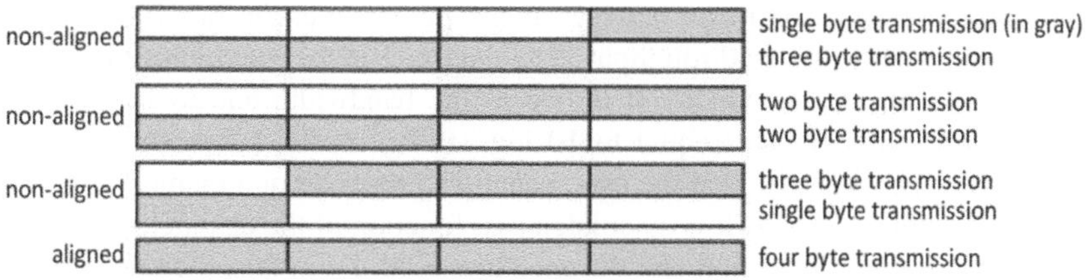

Figure 1.6. *Possible misalignments during the transmission of a 32-bit word (Borrill and Theus 1984)*

The disadvantages of serial transmission tend to be the advantages of parallel transmission, and vice versa. In absolute terms, parallel communication is n times faster than its counterpart (for k = 1) for a set clock rate. The bitrate can be increased simply by widening the bus. There is no (de)serialization time. The synchronization signals are additional signals, increasing its width correspondingly. There is therefore no overhead in terms of bitrate. However, the connection cost (cable, PCB and connector) is greater than for its counterpart as it takes up more space. Dealing with errors is also more complicated. The problem of clock skew between signals (line-to-line skew) has to be considered for high bitrates (*cf.* § 3.5.3 in Darche (2004) and § 3.6.6 and 7.1.2 in Darche (2012)). Progress in fast electronics means that nowadays the serial link is adequate for most bitrate requirements. Moreover, it is becoming widespread in computers, replacing buses with simpler point-to-point connections. The link is made up of a pair of one-directional channels of opposing directions. This is referred to as a link or lane, for example the PCI Express bus (PCI-E or PCIe), described in Jackson and Budruk (2012).

The flow of information is measured in number of bits, or multiples thereof (usually bytes), transmitted per unit of time. It is a function of the information format n. The base unit is the bit per second (bit/s, b/s or bps), and its multiples are powers of 10 ($\times\ 10^{3\ \times\ k}$, $k \in \mathbb{N}^*$). In increasing order, there is the kilobit/s (kbit/s = 10^3 bit/s or kbps), the megabit/s (Mbit/s = 10^6 bit/s or Mbps), the gigabit/s (Gbit/s = 10^9 bit/s or Gbps) and the terabit/s (Tbit/s or 10^{12} bit/s or Tbps). These units[7] are mostly used for networks. The bit per second is the equivalent to a baud for a valency of 2. For the bus and the interfaces, we can also use the byte per second (B/s) and multiples thereof, such as the kilobyte/s (kB/s = 10^3 bytes/s), the megabyte/s (MB/s = 10^6 bytes/s), the gigabyte/s (GB/s = 10^9 bytes/s) and the terabyte/s (TB/s = 10^{12} bytes/s). A dedicated bus provides a higher bitrate than its generic alternative, and handling the electronics is simpler, especially for the controller and interface electronics. It is more costly in terms of connections, however.

A distinction must be made between two types of rate: the raw bitrate or data rate, and the useful rate or throughput. The data rate is the maximum rate that the bus is able to physically handle. It is tied to the bandwidth and to the Signal-to-Noise Ratio (SNR, which is equal to 10 $\log_{10}(P_s/P_n)$ in dB) (Shannon 1948). The throughput is the mean rate that the user, usually a processor or a memory controller, will be able to make use of. It is calculated as a function of the channel's bandwidth, the format n of the information and the encoding used. From this, the rate relating to handling the data rate communication is subtracted. We can thus define the efficiency of a bus η as the ratio of the number of useful bits to the total bits in the message. There is also the burst transfer rate (*cf.* § 2.2). Moreover, there can also be transfer modes like the Double Data Rate (DDR) or Quad Data Rate (QDR), as there is for Random Access Memory (RAM, *cf.* § 4.6.2 and 6.5 in Darche (2012)), where each edge of the transmission clock transmits one piece of information, thus theoretically doubling, or respectively quadrupling, the data rate.

A bus is said to be passive if it contains no active electronic components (i.e. transistors or diodes). It simply ensures the connection between elements of the bus. Figure 1.7 gives two examples of this. From left to right, it shows an I/O bus unit with Hard Disk Drives (HDD), by Integrated Drive Electronics (Schmidt 1995) in the form of a flat cable and of a backplane bus (*cf.* § 4.2.7). An example of this last item

7 The prefixes of these units must not be confused with those used for measuring the size of a memory, which we recall are: kilo (= 2^{10}), mega (= 2^{20}), giga (= 2^{30}) and tera (= 2^{40}), *cf.* § I-2.6.1 in Darche (2000)). There was some ambiguity surrounding the corresponding symbols. Only kilo could be represented with capital K, and all the others had to be determined based on the context. Fortunately, these prefixes have since be standardized by the IEEE ((IEEE 2002a b), *cf.* § V1-2.1 and § 1.1 in Darche (2012)).

was bus S-100[8], standardized under reference ANSI/IEEE Std 696-1983 (ANSI/IEEE 1982b). Otherwise, it is said to be active. The driver is tasked with amplifying the signals and controlling the bus. Other technologies that can be utilized are radiofrequencies, infrared or even lighting technologies (laser). These are limited to wireless connections. Optics is a possible next step for buses, but this is still in the research phase, although they are starting to be used in the extension bus and the I/O bus. Savage (2002) develops this approach further. A major obstacle is cost and the need to convert optical/electrical signals.

A bus is said to be external when it is located outside the computer. This is nearly always an I/O bus (*cf.* § 4.2.6). Otherwise, it is internal. The SCSI (Small Computer System Interface) I/O bus could be both internal and external. Internally, it linked the mass storage units. Externally, it could exist as part of peripherals such as a printer or a scanner (*cf.* respectively § 6.3 and 5.3.1 in Darche (2003)).

a) **b)**

Figure 1.7. *Ribbon-cable I/O bus (IDE) and a backplane bus. For a color version of this figure, see www.iste.co.uk/darche/microprocessor2.zip*

Bus mechanics relate to all aspects of the assembly of components and printed circuits, as well as all aspects of connection. Bus mechanics specify, among other things, the maximum length of the bus, specifications of the connector/s and, potentially, the size and fixation type of the electronic card (motherboard, daughterboard or expansion card) and of the housing, cabinet or rack that houses them. The connector specifications state their maximum number, size, position, distance between two connectors, and their interconnection gap, etc. The connectors of an expansion bus, if installed onto a printed circuit like in the motherboard of a micro-computer, take up a significant amount of space (1/4th to 1/3rd of the surface

8 Bus S-100 takes its name from the number of lines it contains. It was first used in the kit micro-computer Altair 8800 (8-bit Intel 8080 microprocessor, main memory with 256 bytes of RAM, with possible expansion to 64 KiB) from the company MITS (Micro Instrumentation Telemetry Systems), which first appeared on the market in 1975.

area of a personal computer (PC)-type motherboard) and therefore contribute significantly to the overall cost of the system. A bus's connections should not be underestimated as they are without a doubt its weakest link and make it less reliable.

Electrical characteristics relate to the voltages and currents of input, output and I/O, and the minimum, maximum and nominal voltages and currents of the signals (*cf.* § 1.2 and 2.2.1 in Darche (2004)) and of the bus lines. They are primarily those of the logic used (*cf.* Chapter 2 in Darche (2004)). The electrical load, as seen by the emitter, is an important parameter as it directly affects the rise and fall times of the signals. They rely on the bus itself, as well as on the connector, the daughterboard and possibly any stub relaying the bus towards the connector. This load is variable and depends upon, among other things, the number of nodes and whether all the slots are occupied by an inserted electronic card, thus forming a load. Moreover, each connector makes the bus longer by creating a stub that derives the main bus, or "backbone" (Figure 1.8), thus modifying the electrical and temporal characteristics of the bus. This load is complex (mathematically speaking) as it contains resistive, capacitive and inductive components respectively. This derivation can also introduce impedance mismatch, which is a potential source of electrical disturbance due to the reflection of signals at the end of the line. This characteristic should be considered when determining the maximum number of connectable elements.

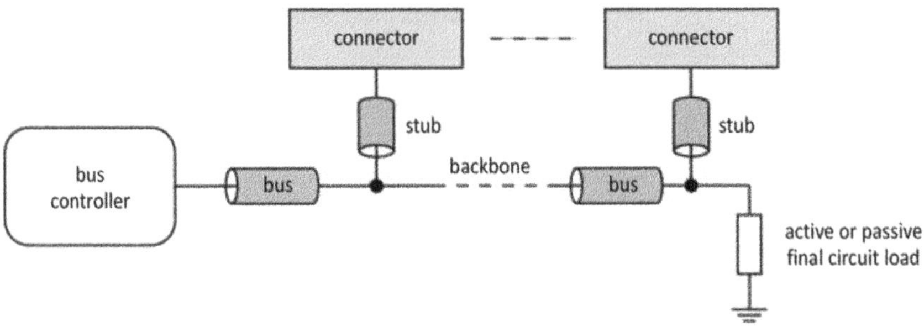

Figure 1.8. *Bus lines and derivation stubs*

The bus also possesses temporal characteristics that are tied to the protocol or to the technology used, such as the rise, fall and propagation times of the signals, and the temporal relations that exist between them. The bus-settling time is the time required for the signal to become stable. Another important time is the flight time t_{flight} (*cf.* § 3.3.4 in Darche (2012), with an example in Intel 97). It is the time taken by a signal to cover the full length of the bus. It takes into consideration all of the propagation times of the interface electronics, any skews and the time window of capture by the receiver. It also includes the bus propagation time t_L (*cf.* § 3.3.1). One empirical rule is that $6 \times t_{flight}$ should be less than 30% of the Unit Interval (UI, or in other words a period of 1 bit) of the eye diagram (or eye pattern, *cf.* § 3.5.3 in Darche (2004) and § 7.1.2 in Darche (2012)) for a stable state at the sampling point at 50%. The protocol also includes delays such as those linked to arbitration.

A bus is poorly scalable, in that the addition of nodes has a negative impact on its electrical and temporal characteristics, limiting it practically. The access time and rate are worsened by distortion and the arbitration time, and the designer must plan for the worst case, which is not very efficient.

SUMMARY.– The advantages of a bus are its versatility and adaptability. New electronic cards can be added to it easily. Cards can be transferred from one computer to another as long as they have the same bus standard and maintenance can be ensured. The computer system itself can be designed to be partitioned. It is relatively inexpensive as it constitutes a primary approach rather than a collection of shared cables or traces. The main disadvantage is that it forms a bottleneck (or tailback) in terms of communication. The bandwidth of a bus limits the I/O data-rate. Other characteristics also limit this rate, such as the length of the bus, as well as the number of nodes. Furthermore, if the nodes are heterogeneous, characteristics such as latency or data transfer speed will be heterogeneous too. Scaling up is just as hard, and can even prove to be impossible.

1.3. Synchronism and asynchrony

Those involved in an exchange must communicate at speeds that are compatible with this exchange. An exchange can be synchronous or asynchronous, depending on whether a clock signal pacing the transfer is explicitly sent or not[9]. In a synchronous bus (with an interconnection), a master clock[10] provides a clock signal that paces and synchronizes the exchanges between elements of the bus. This signal is distributed between all of the nodes of the bus, and is either amplified (radial clock distribution, Figure 1.9(a)) or not (bussed clock distribution, Figure 1.9(b)), with each node able to generate a local clock. The problems associated with the clock are temporal in nature (e.g. skew, jitter, noise, etc.), but can also be electrical, such as metastability, for example, the criticality of which is directly proportional to the frequency. Moreover, the user module (*cf.* § 3.1) can either use this signal or have its own clocks.

---

9 Synchronization through software can be a convention of characters, such as the Xon–Xoff protocol, for example, or a known or given frame length. It cannot be used for buses due to low efficiency.

10 Continuous time can be considered, as shown in Del Corso *et al.* (1986), but in practice, event discretization is preferred.

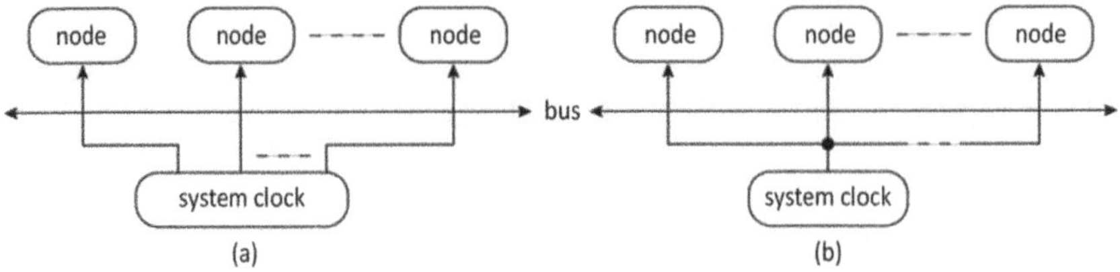

Figure 1.9. *Distribution of the (a) radial or (b) bussed clock signal*

Each operation has to be carried out within a constant time interval that is tied to its period. Otherwise, a transfer error takes place. In nearly all cases, the signal in a bus is handled by the edge of an active clock (this is an edge-triggered logic model), marking the start of an exchange. However, a level-sensitive logic model can also be considered. Figure 1.10 shows the causal link between signals, with an example of an exchange request with a read receipt provided. In the purely synchronous model, no cycle start signal is needed as it is the active clock edge that marks this start. The time characteristics are fixed. The period of the clock signal must therefore be greater than the propagation time of the bus plus any times relating to the logic, such as the setup time t_{setup}.

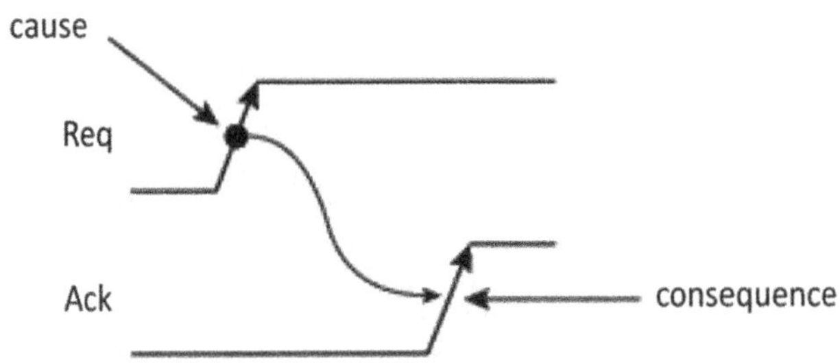

Figure 1.10. *Causal link between signals*

The cadencing diagrams are asynchronous or synchronous, classical or derived, mesochronous[11] or plesiochronous. In a mesochronous system, local clocks are derived from a global clock. Delays in the transfer of clock signals are not even, resulting in phase shifts. A mesochronous system is said to be "static" when the phase difference between clock signals of the same frequency does not vary during system operation. A "dynamic mesochronous system" exists when this phase difference varies for each component, for example, because of temperature or supply

11 From the Greek root "meso", meaning "in the middle of".

voltage variations. An example of such a system is the basic Rambus channel (*cf.* § 7.2.1 in Darche (2012)). If the clocks are independent and not synchronized but the average frequency is the same, so with a slight drift, the communication is said to be "plesiochronous[12]". An example is the RS-232 series interface (*cf.* § 8.2.2 in Darche (2003)). When the frequencies are different, the communication is said to be "heterochronous[13]". More details on synchronization can be found in Messerschmitt (1990).

Designing a synchronous system is harder than designing an asynchronous one. The clock domains and of their interactions must be taken into account (Clock Domain Crossing, CDC). The problem has been covered in sections § 3.6.6 and 7.1.2 of Darche (2012). A purely synchronous system carries out one transaction per clock period. This is called a bus cycle. This is not the case in a semi-synchronous system (also called pseudo-synchronous or clocked), which is instead characterized by a longer time interval, the bus cycle of which is a multiple of the system clock period. This number of periods can be fixed, limited or free. During a transaction, transmission can become asynchronous through the help of a wait request signal (the Wait signal, for example), adding clock cycles in order to lengthen the transaction. An example of a semi-synchronous bus is the NuBus (TI 1983). A variation of this is source-synchronous clocking (*cf.* § 7.1.2 in Darche (2012)). An example of a synchronous bus is the Multibus II backplane bus from the company Intel, standardized through the reference ANSI/IEEE Std 1296 (IEEE 1988).

The asynchronous bus represents a different approach, the advantage of which is that a global clock signal is not used, which can be limiting in terms of design time. The dedicated time slot can be made longer as needed. Thus, exchange times can be adapted to the speed of the nodes. However, there is a risk of blocking the exchange if there is no limit to the response time, as a new cycle cannot begin if the previous one has not finished. This means that the bus can remain indefinitely allocated to the master that holds it. Two examples of asynchronous buses are the Unibus™ backplane bus from the company Digital Equipment Corporation (DEC) and the Multibus I from Intel, standardized through reference ANSI/IEEE Std 796 (ANSI/IEEE 1982a).

In terms of asynchronous protocols, the first group is those with one-way control, that is, controlled by a single component of the exchange. This is referred to as a "One-Way Command", or OWC. It is simple, with a single Req(uest) (the forward signal). Figure 1.11 highlights this through the reading of a piece of information. The request signal is activated (timestamp 1). Next is the positioning of the information by the source S after a certain amount of access time t_a

12 From the Greek root "plesio" meaning "neighbor".

13 From the Greek root "hetero" meaning "different".

(timestamp 2). When the request is deactivated (timestamp 3), the information is removed by the slave source S (timestamp 4). The temporal characteristics of the bus, in particular the propagation delay t_{pd}, must be considered in order to quantify the access time t_a. In this version, the transfer time is adapted to the requester as it is the latter that (de)activates the request signal ("destination-controlled transfer"). The main disadvantage is that there is no check for the validity of the exchange by the destination D. If the source fails, it cannot carry it out. Note that time t_{dis} (dis for disable) qualifies the deactivation time of the three-state electronic buffers (*cf.* § 3.3.4)

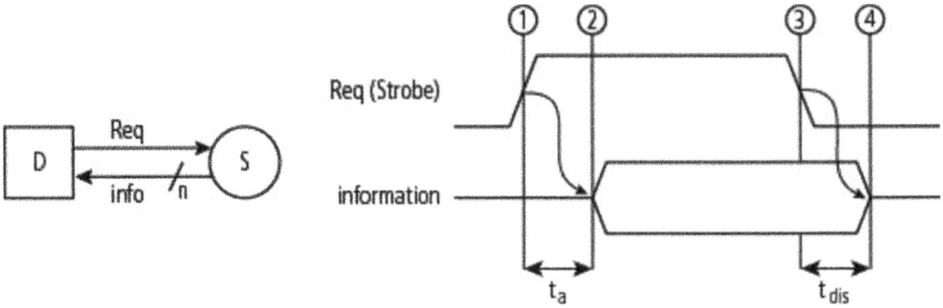

Figure 1.11. *One-way control protocol*

Another term used to refer to one-way control is "strobe protocol", as shown in Figure 1.12, which highlights the transmission of a piece of data (source-controlled transfer). After a certain data setup time t_{setup} (timestamp 1), the emitter signals its presence (timestamp 2) and its retreat (timestamp 3), which becomes effective during step 4. The limits of this protocol are seen again in the transmission of a data item when there is a transfer error if the receiver is not listening or does not account for it sufficiently quickly.

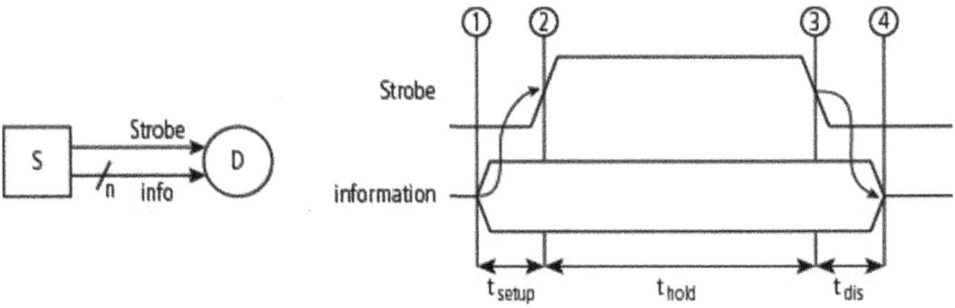

Figure 1.12. *Strobe protocol*

The handshake protocol was created as a solution to the downsides of the strobe protocol. It is the most common protocol among unclocked systems (also known as clockless, or self-timed systems), and is source-controlled. In a master/slave setup, a master M sends a request to the slave S, which must answer. It uses two signals, which are a Req(uest) and an Ack(nowledgment). The former is used as part of the signaling, while the latter is a backward signal. As there are two signals, the protocol is said to be one of double-track handshake signaling. These signals can be asserted or non-asserted. A Comp(letion) signal marks the end of processing. Depending on the presence and direction(s) of the transmission of information (Figure 1.13), the signal can exist in one of two versions, with either two or four phases, and with four different channels, which are nonput, push, pull and biput The nonput channel (a) does not exchange data, but rather allows for synchronization between the communicating elements. The push channel (b) sends data, while the pull channel (c) receives it. The biput channel (d) is bidirectional. The black dot in the figure means that the entity is active in terms of communication, while a hollow dot means that it is passive. A functioning module can be integrated into the channel as an element of combinational logic – the whole forms a stage of the pipeline (*cf.* § 4.5.1 and 6.1 in Darche (2012) and V2 on future microprocessors).

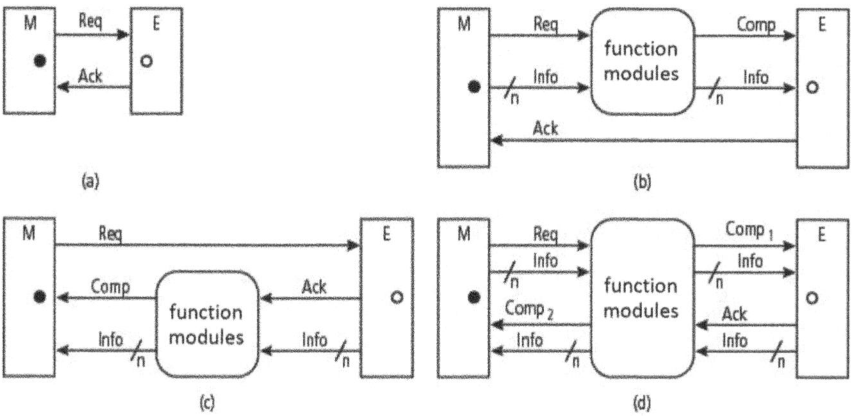

Figure 1.13. *The four possible channels of the handshake protocol*

There are three different versions of this protocol depending on the position of the synchronization signals: non-interlocked, half-interlocked and complete. Complete interlocking means that no more exchanges can take place as long as the previous one is not yet finished and signaled. In the two-phase handshaking version, shown in Figure 1.1.4, there are two types of exchange, which are the "up" handshake, which uses the Req↑ and Ack↑ signals, and the "down" handshake, which uses signals Req↓ and Ack↓. For each of them, there are two transitions, or phases, embodied by the edges of the request signal Req and the receipt acknowledgment signal Ack. The level of the signals is therefore irrelevant, as opposed to the rising or falling edges (this is "edge-sensitive" control, or transition signaling), which are significant (it is an "event-based" protocol), hence the term "two-stroke" signaling (or two-cycle signaling, transition, Non-Return-(to-)Zero (NRZ)). At the end of the exchange, these two signals are in the same state, whereas during the exchange, they were in opposite states. There is an initialization state, which is the transition of the reception signal, here Ack↓, which sets off the exchange (dashed line). Note that the acknowledgment signal can be complemented.

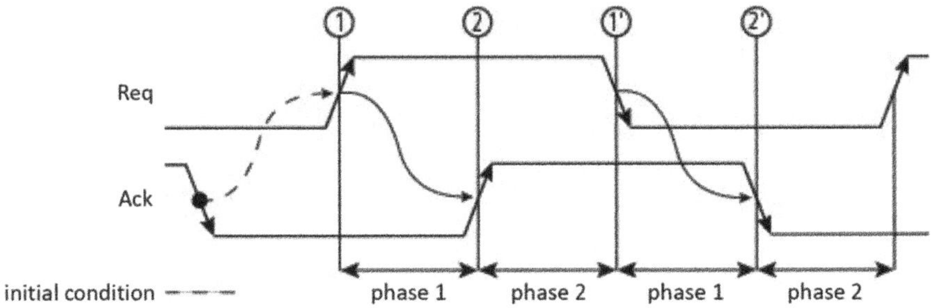

Figure 1.14. *Rising and falling versions of the two-phase handshake protocol*

In the case of a push channel (Figure 1.15), once the information has been positioned, a request is sent out in the form of a transition of request signal Req. When the receiver has processed the information, it signals for it through a transition of the acknowledgment signal Ack.

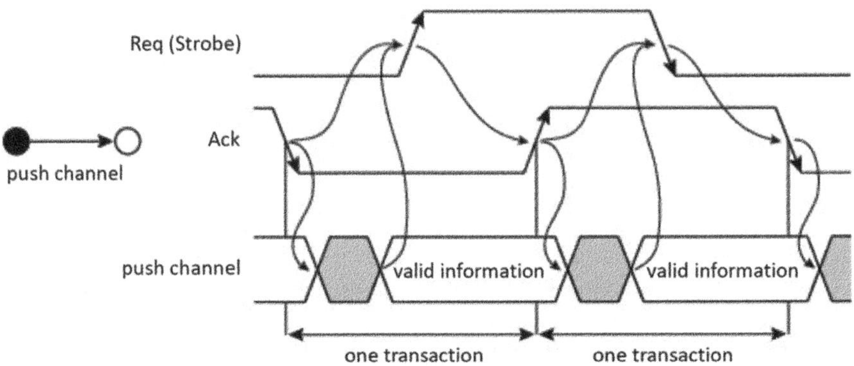

Figure 1.15. *Two-phase handshake in a push channel*

In the case of a pull channel (Figure 1.16), the request leads to the information being positioned by the source, which then signals for it through an acknowledgment.

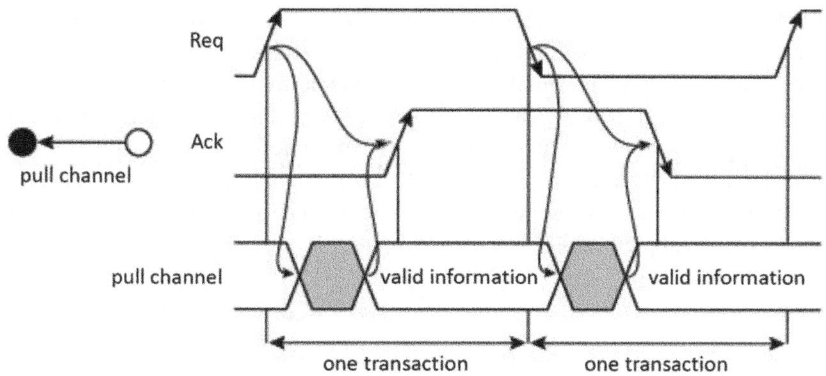

Figure 1.16. *Two-phase handshake in a pull channel*

Note that there is an overlapping of data validity between the two previous channel types during a transaction, as shown in the two gray vertical areas in Figure 1.17.

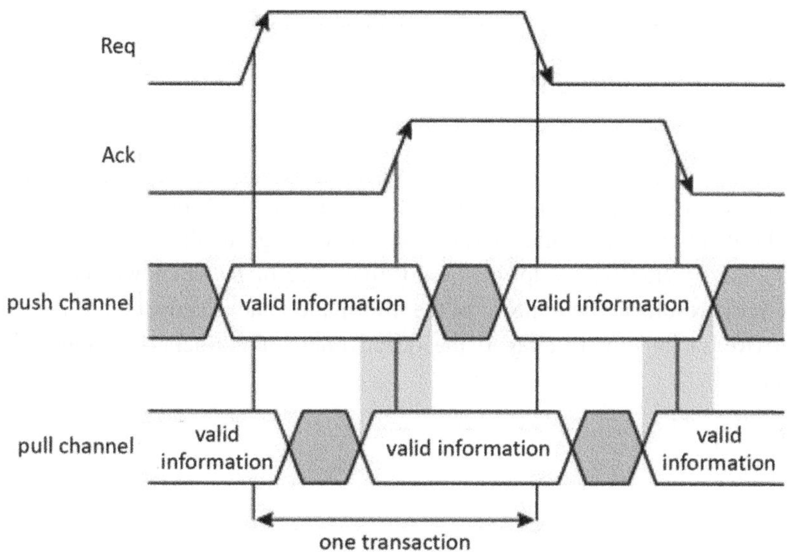

Figure 1.17. *Validity overlapping between the two channels*

In order to eliminate the toggle circuit during hardware implementation, a four-phase handshake protocol is required, also known as double-handshaking. Here, the level of the signals is significant (level-sensitive control). In the complete interlocking version shown in Figure 1.18, there are two types of exchange, which are the up handshake and the descendent handshake. For each of these, there are two transitions, or phases, which are embodied by the edges of the request signal Req and the acknowledgment signal Ack, hence the term four-stroke (or four-cycle) signaling. At the end of the exchange, these two signals return to their initial state 0, while during the two phases, they were in opposite states. For this reason, the double handshake is called "Return-(To-)Zero (R(T)Z)" signaling. An initial state is an equilibrium of the states of the protocol signals. The dashed line in Figure 1.18 represents an example of this.

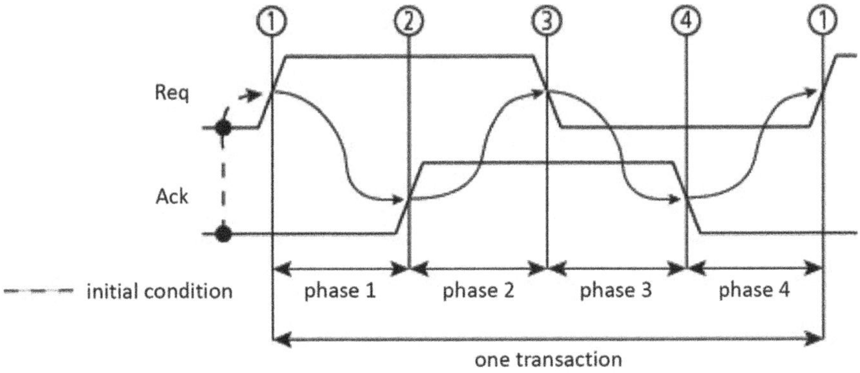

Figure 1.18. *Four-phase handshake protocol*

For a push channel, the Req and Ack signals respectively mean valid data (Strobe) and a completion signal. As shown in Figure 1.19, the emitter signals the availability of the information through the rising edge of the strobe signal Req[14] (Req↑). As previously, receipt of the positive edge of the acknowledgment signal Acq (Ack↑) results in the removal of the information and deactivation of the request signal (Req↓), in turn leading to the deactivation of the acknowledgment signal (Ack↓).

14 Colmenar *et al.* (2009) starts the transaction one phase earlier, that is, at Ack↓.

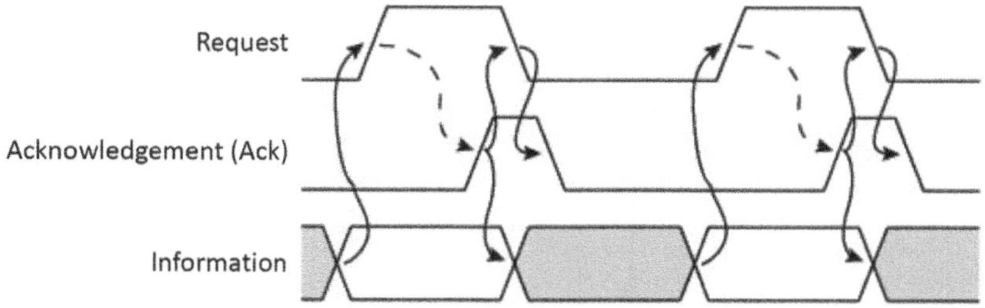

Figure 1.19. *Four-phase handshake protocols for a push channel (Darche 2012)*

There are actually four versions of this channel: (Figure 1.20) early (Furber and Day 1996; Furber and Liu 1996), broadish (or extended early), broad and late. For the first three, there is valid data on the rising edge of the Req request – it is therefore the invalidation of this data that differentiates them according to the three edge possibilities. The data is no longer valid on the rising edge of the acknowledgement signal for the early mode, on the falling edge of the request signal for the broadish mode, and on the falling edge of the acknowledgement signal for the broad and late modes. For the late mode, the data is valid on the falling edge of the request signal.

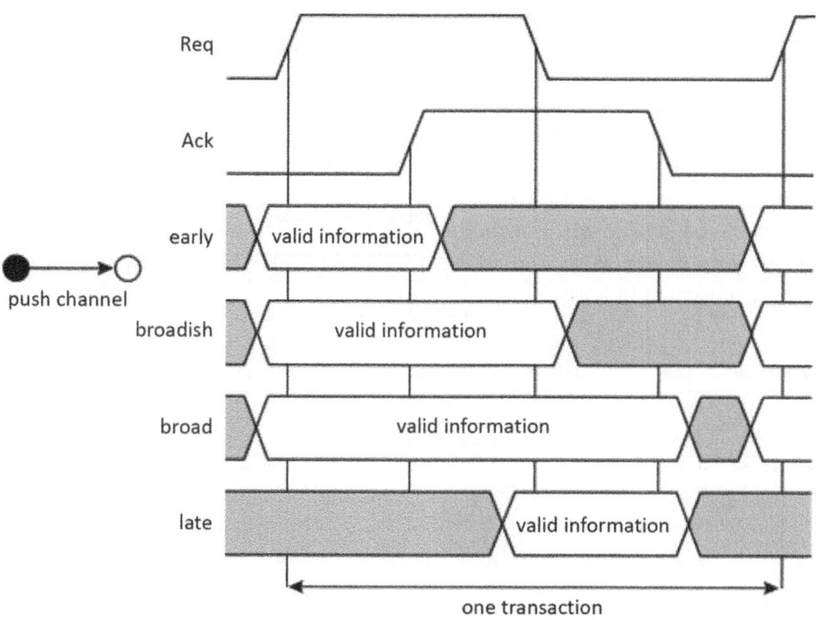

Figure 1.20. *Four versions of the four-phase handshake protocol for a push channel*

Figure 1.21 shows the "data request" version (pull channel), again with the four variations.

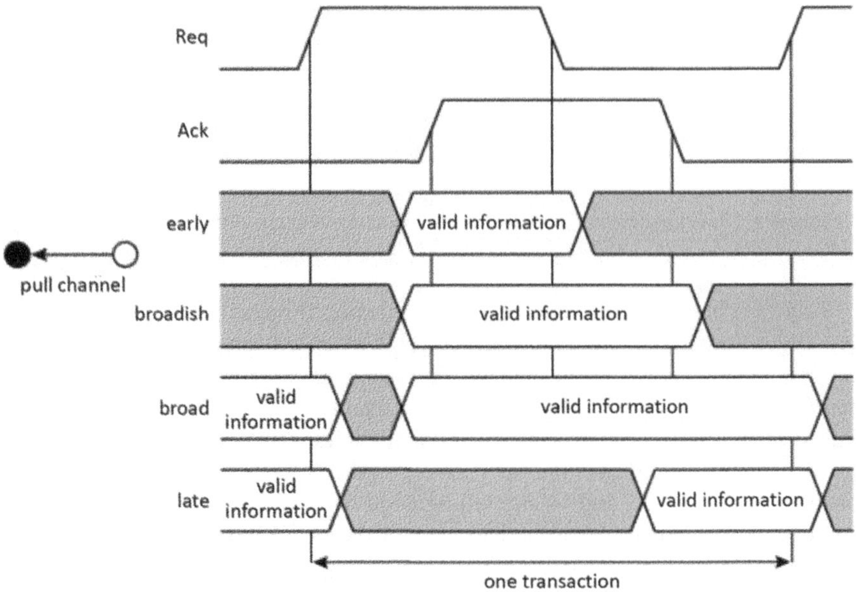

Figure 1.21. *Four versions of the four-phase handshake protocol for a pull channel*

Figure 1.22 shows the other two possible versions of the handshake protocol, which are "half-interblocked" and "non-interblocked". The causality of the exchanged is indicated with arrows. The second version is pulse-based signaling, active on the edge or levels, a technique that is similar to transition-based signaling. The operating mode was studied by McCluskey (1962) and his asynchronous version is presented in Nyström and Martin (2002).

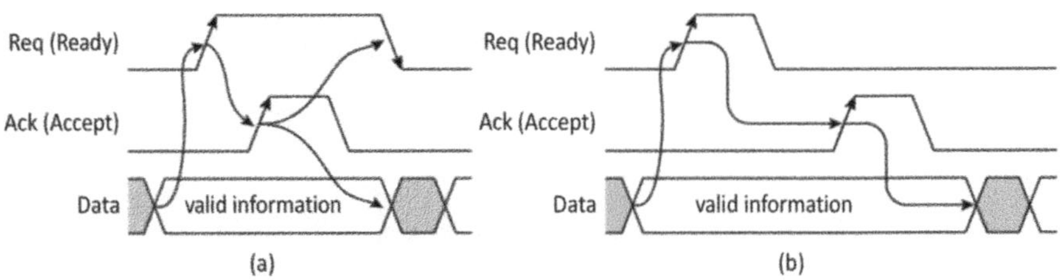

Figure 1.22. *Half-interblocked (a) and non-interblocked (b) handshakes (Thurber et al. 1972)*

Figure 1.23 shows how this can be applied through two examples, a read (a) and a write (b), both asynchronous, carried out by the CPU (Central Processing Unit). The R/#W (Read/#Write) signal is not shown so as to not overload the illustration.

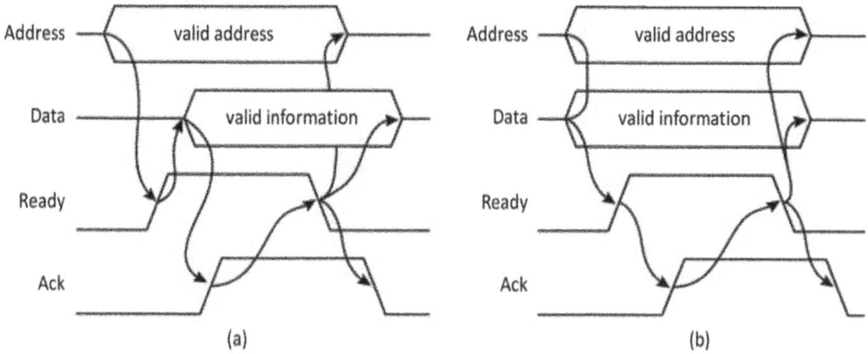

Figure 1.23. *Exchanges between CPU and the memory through a handshake*

To summarize, the OWC and handshake protocols are used by the asynchronous and semi-synchronous buses. The two-phase handshake is quicker than the four-phase, and requires less current in CMOS logic (Complementary Metal Oxide Semiconductor, *cf.* § 2.4 in Darche (2004)). It is particularly well suited for slow communicating systems (Renaudin 2000). The two Req and Ack signals can alternatively be carried through a single cable. This approach was named single-track handshake signaling by Van Berkel and Bink (1996), and its study goes beyond the scope of this work.

1.4. Coding data

The validity of the transmitted data is inherent to the synchronous protocol, as data and validity are correlated. There are several solutions for carrying out validation in an asynchronous protocol. The first is called bundled data. The term comes from Sutherland (1989, 2007), and leads on to the notion of bundling constraint, which forces the data to accurately consider this constraint before proceeding to signaling. A done signal accompanies the transfer of information and validates the information. A superior solution to this is the use of protocol signals Req and Ack as well as the handshake. A single cable is used to transfer a bit of data, hence the notion of single-rail data encoding. For the coding to not be affected by the propagation delay, unlike in the first solution, the coding can be carried out in three or four states. This coding uses two cables (two rails) to encode the value of the validity of the data. This constitutes a robust end solution that is dependent on the data but requires an associated detection logic (*cf.* exercise E1.1). Three-state encoding is governed by the truth table shown in Table 1.1. It is called Dual-Rail (DR) data encoding. This type of approach can be generalized to n number of rails (Multi-Rail or MRn) while working in base n. For example, DR is MR2 encoding. Four-state encoding is governed by the same truth table shown in Table 1.1. The first bit gives the binary value and the second bit gives the logical parity (*cf.* § III.6.6 in Darche (2000)). We can also see that any change along the second rail marks a new bit. Note that the dual-rail code is also called 1-of-2 code, and is part of the 1-of-n codes, that is, the one-hot codes with a size of n, who themselves belong to the m-of-n code family.

Code words (format n = 2)	States in a three-state dual-rail code	States in a four-state dual-rail code
0 0	Invalid or reset	0 even
0 1	0	0 uneven
1 0	1	1 uneven
1 1	Not used	1 even

Table 1.1. *Interpretation of code words in three- and four-state dual-rail codes*

Another aspect of coding relates to the current consumption. Yand *et al.* (2004) suggests encoding the most frequent bit patterns that circulate around the data bus in order to reduce the current consumption of the electronic buffers. This approach was already suggested for solid-state memories with the bus invert by Stan and Burleson (1995), and is further explored in the second volume on future memory devices.

In the microprocessor, the instructions can also be encoded (*cf.* § V4-1.1.1).

1.5. Communication protocol

In order to exchange information, first a *communication protocol* must be defined that can manage this exchange. A protocol is a set of conditions and operations, whose order must be strictly respected for the transaction to take place. The rules to follow for the signals are physical specifications (electrical values) and time and causality constraints of the operations. The operations are the activation or non-activation (by level or by edge) of signals of state, control, and address and data positioning. When a master accesses a slave, it states the type of access, read or write of a word, read or write of a block (in a block transfer), Read–Modify–Write (RMW mode) or a word, writing after reading (write-after-read mode) or access in interruption mode (address-only and interrupt acknowledge cycles. RMW mode allows for synchronization and locking mechanisms to be implemented, such as the semaphore, or lower down, the `test-and-set` instruction (*cf.* § V4-2.6.1). The two main corresponding control signals (*cf.* § 3.2) are read enable or signalization signals (#R, #RE (E for Enable), #Rd or #RS (S for Signal)) and the same for write (#W, #WE, #Wr or #WS). There are also spatial characteristics that specify the information to be exchanged, and in the case of communication through bundles, the structure of the messages (especially the size). If communication is carried out through a datagram (i.e. a message), the protocol specifies its size (unit: bit or byte) and its structure, that is, the different fields (spatial characteristics), as well as the length and sequencing (temporal characteristics).

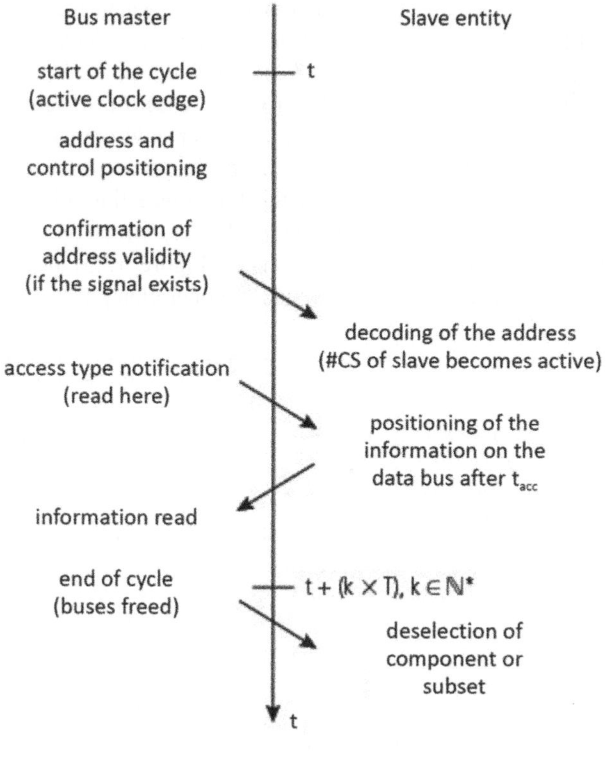

Figure 1.24. *Sequencing diagram of a synchronous read*

Figure 1.24 shows a synchronous operation, with a master, in this case, a processor, carrying out a read operation in a memory device. The arrow points to an action or cause that implies a new signal condition. The transfer is said to be addressed, as the correspondent is unique and chosen by the address. It sends the address along the address bus, which is subsequently taken into account by all of the address decoders (*cf.* § 2.2.2 in Darche (2003)) of the slave entities. The entity involved is accessed through activation of its selection signal (CS signal for *Chip Select* or CE for *Chip Enable*)) and send the desired data back. Remember that everything is synchronized to a clock and that the cycle has a duration of $k \times T$, $k \in \mathbb{N}^*$, with T the period of the clock. The synchronous protocol is deterministic.

It is possible to functionally split a cycle, referred to as a "transaction". This term refers to a coherent unit during processing, which can be decomposed into an ordered sequence of unitary tasks. It is the logical activity unit of the bus or bus cycle that takes the form of a sequence of signals. This sequence follows rule flows that are gathered together in a communication protocol. If a clock synchronizes the operation of a bus, then the transaction takes places during one (in the case of a synchronous bus), or several bus cycles (in the case of a semi- or pseudo-synchronous bus). Only in the case of a multi-master environment does the clock start with an access request, followed by an arbitration phase (also called selection phase) between those requesting access to the bus. Once this arbitration phase is over, the chosen one then engages in the exchange, which is divided into an addressing phase, an information transfer phase (Figure 1.25) or even, in more complex protocols, an error detection and signaling operation phase.

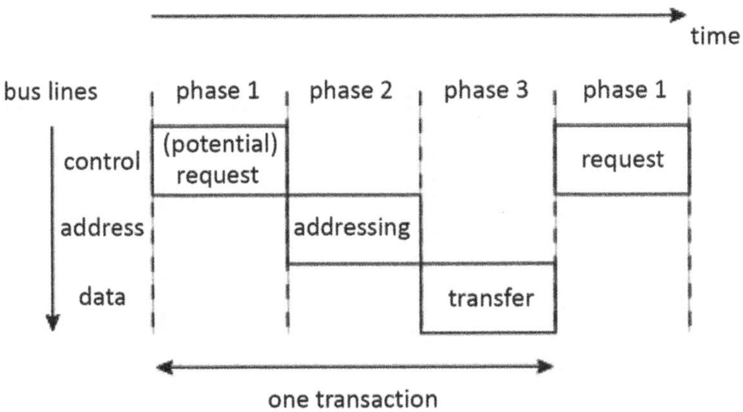

Figure 1.25. *A bus transaction*

There are four fundamental pieces of information that must pass through the bus: the addresses of the source and of the destination, the information being transported and the operation that is to be executed. Usually, the source address is implicit. The information to be transferred is typically a machine instruction, data or an address, but it can also be a command, control, state or an interruption request or associated vector, etc. Note also that the addressing phase can be prolonged during the transfer phase, thus blocking the address bus, most likely unnecessarily. The issue can be addressed by transforming the read operation into a write operation for the case of a transfer between I/O controllers, or between the bus bridge, as proposed by Okazawa *et al.* (1998). The operation to be executed is a read, a write or a read–modify–write, but there are also special cycles (*cf.* § 2.2). In terms of the slave, the phases of access request, address decoding and transfer will take place in succession. A bus initialization phase is potentially required in order to power on the calculator or on demand. This involves ordering the powering on or off of the modules, in a set order if required, and to place them in a known state.

We can now establish the chronogram presented in Figure 1.26, which relates to the exchange as seen by the microprocessor. The access time t_{ACC} is the minimum time needed before the data can be processed. t_{DSR} is the data setup time that takes place before the microprocessor can begin processing. Note that there is a data hold time at the end of each cycle, t_{DHR} or t_{DHW} depending on the operation, and t_{AH} for the address. A synchronous transfer is faster. It makes design easier (simple logic) and guarantees exchange times. However, for this to happen, all elements of the bus have to work at the same frequency. The main principle of synchronous communication is strict adherence to the times, without which there is a risk of transfer errors. The cycle length t_{cyc}, in particular, is fixed.

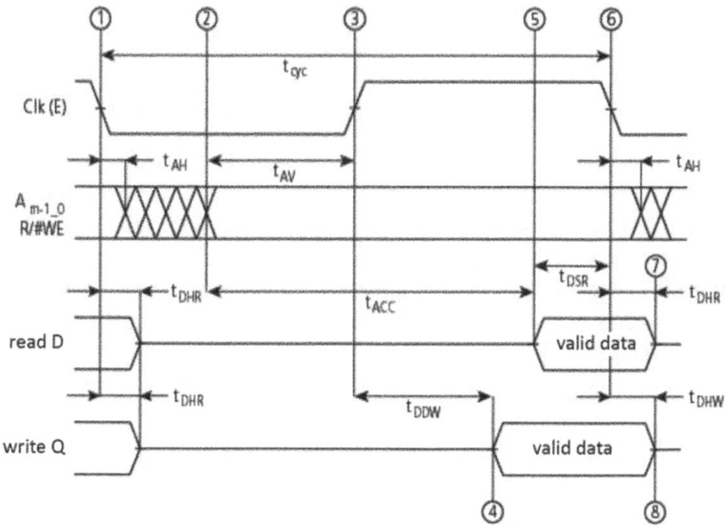

Figure 1.26. *Simplified chronograms of synchronous read and write operations in the MC6802 microprocessor*

Figure 1.27 gives an example of read access for a microprocessor using a multiplexed address/data bus. The ALE signal (Address Latch Enable) signals the presence of a valid address on the bus. The exchange type is “relaxed synchronous” as the cycle is prolonged by several reference clock periods, depending on the state of the Ready signal. In this synchronous version, the length a memory access time is measured in bus cycles, with one bus cycle being made of a number of clock cycles. More generally, the number of cycles depends on the length m of the data bus, the format n of the information and whether the access or information is aligned or not.

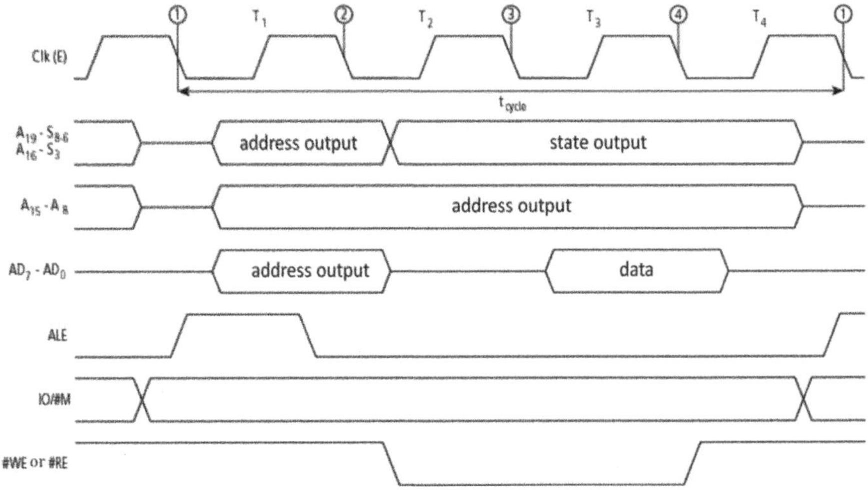

Figure 1.27. *Read cycle with address/data multiplexing (iAPX88 microprocessor from Intel)*

The alternative is an asynchronous operation. This has the advantages of reduced current consumption, which is vital in mobile systems, and greater flexibility in terms of design. However, there is no time guarantee, and specific transfer protocols, based on handshaking (*cf.* § 1.3), for example, must be established. Figure 1.28 shows a four-phase handshake.

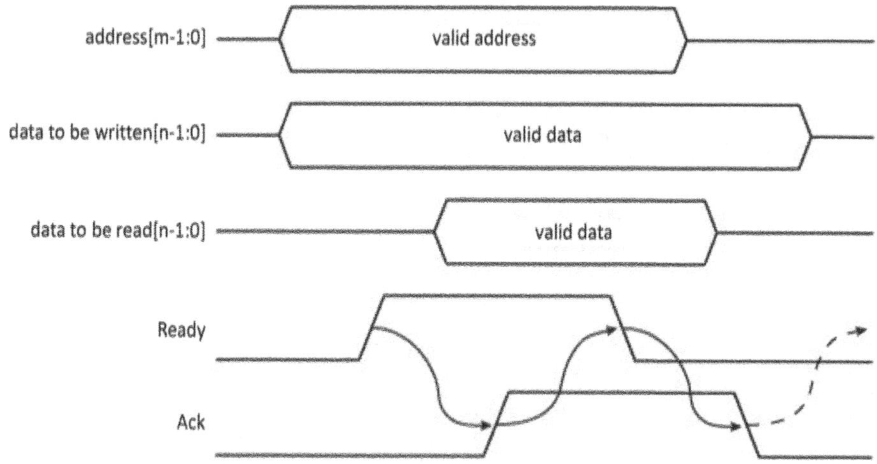

Figure 1.28. *Read or write cycle with a four-phase handshake*

The first one uses two signals, a strobe signal (Ready, in this case) and an acknowledgment signal, which enables a feedback signal. The transaction requires the bus to be crossed twice, thus slowing the exchange, as this is one more than in the synchronous version. During an asynchronous operation, the beginning of the protocol is the same as previously described, except that the reading of the data is tied to an acknowledgment signal from the slave (e.g. the -DTAck signal from the MPU MC68000 by Motorola). It is possible for the signal to not arrive, thus blocking the exchange, and consequently the bus (Figure 1.29). Mechanisms like the watchdog (*cf.* § V3-5.3 and § 3.3.1 in Darche (2003)) can unblock this situation, generating a bus error in the form of a Negative Acknowledgment (NK), through a third-party component, for example. A lack of addressable components can easily be detected, as it is given away by the lack of response.

The advantage of asynchronous communication is the ability to mix slow elements with faster ones on the same bus without any specific adaptations. The fast elements adapt to the speed of the others ("leveling down").

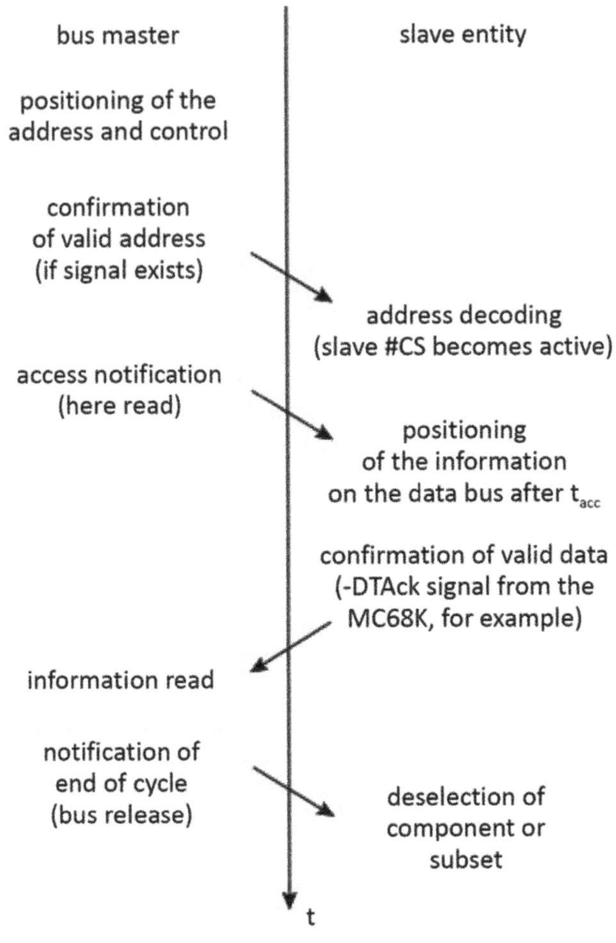

Figure 1.29. *Diagram of an asynchronous read sequence*

Figure 1.30 presents a completely asynchronous read by the MC68000 microprocessor. Once the address has been positioned, the #AS (Address Strobe) signal marks the start of the bus cycle. The read/write (R/W) signal is activated for one read. The slave activates the #DTAck signal in order to tell the MPU that the data to be read has been positioned on the bus. The #UDS/#LDS (Upper/Lower Data Strobe) signals let us choose the format of the operation. In these chronograms, we can recognize a handshake with interblocking (*cf.* 1.3), where the Req/Ack signals are represented by #AS/#DTAck, which are active in the low state. A more complete version can be found in Figure V3-2.20.

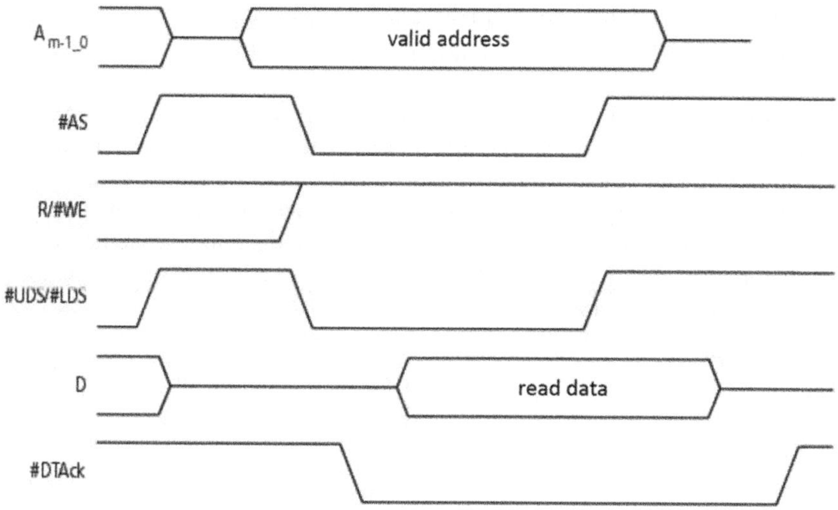

Figure 1.30. *Asynchronous read cycle in the MC68000 microprocessor*

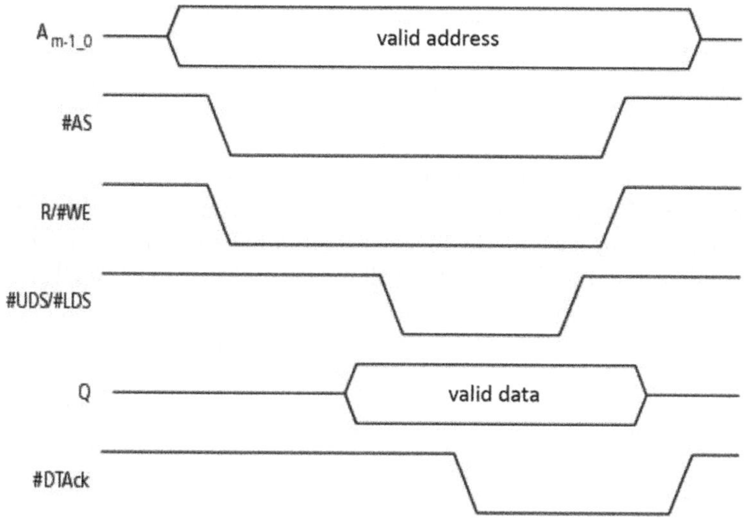

Figure 1.31. *Asynchronous write cycle in the MC68000 microprocessor*

An asynchronous write cycle (Figure 1.31) starts, as previously, with the activation of the #AS and write signals. The data is positioned by the CPU, which signals by activating the #UDS/#LDS signals, which mark its validity. A more complete version of this is the one shown in Figure V3-2.20.

An example of a semi-synchronous transfer is the one presented in Figure 1.32, which shows a memory access through a "transputer", a microprocessor from the company Inmos Ltd (taken over by STMicroelectronics). One read cycle normally takes place over six half-periods; here, it is made longer by adding a half-period of waiting W, as sampling of the state of the delay signal is done on the falling clock edge, before the end of cycle T4. The events are discretized here. The number of half-periods added is limited physically.

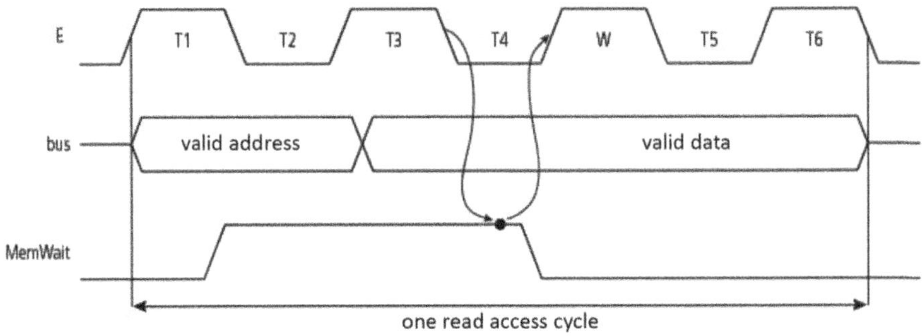

Figure 1.32. *Simplified chronograms of an asynchronous read by transputer*

Other variations of cycle lengthening can be considered. One example is shown in Figure 1.33 where the wait request signal must remain active for the amount of time needed for propagation. The time is here said to be continuous, as there is no clock signal interfering. The Wait signal allows the exchange to be lengthened.

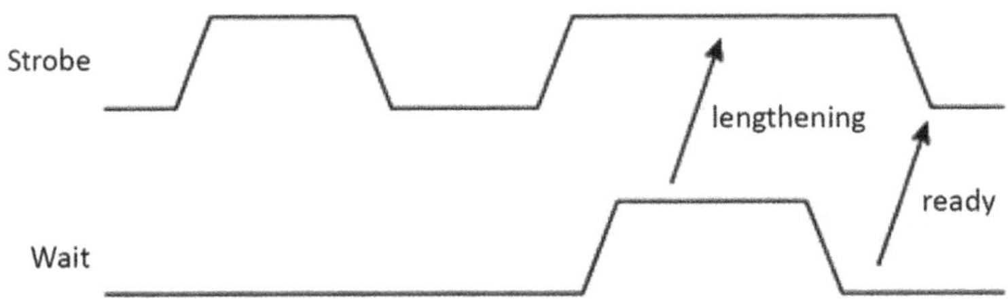

Figure 1.33. *Lengthening a cycle with the handshake (from Nicoud (1987))*

Another variation, still of the "handshake" type, is presented in Figure 1.34. It is run in 32-bit microprocessors, where a positive acknowledgment ends the exchange. In the case where the slave cannot satisfy the request, a negative acknowledgment

NAck is sent. In this way, the handshake is able to carry out flow control. It is said to be bounded.

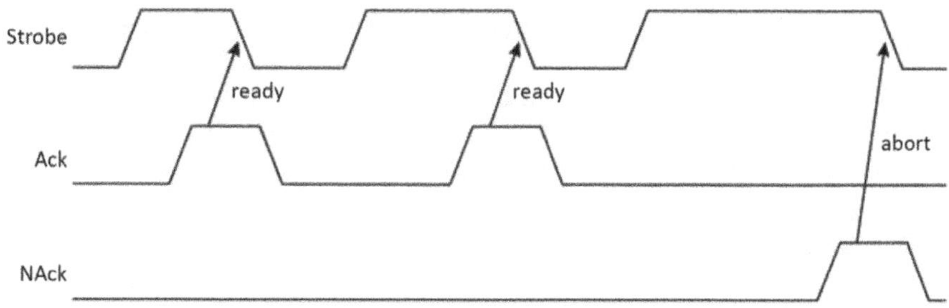

Figure 1.34. *Lengthening a cycle with positive and negative acknowledgments (from Nicoud (1987))*

An addressed selection involves providing an address or a range of addresses to a slave. An addressed transfer involves providing an address which will then be decoded in order to select (i.e. activate) a slave. Typically, the slave has defined addresses. One variation is geographical addressing, which tells us which card is currently occupying a given slot. For this, each slot is attributed a number, called a slot space, and each connector is given an equal addressing zone. The most significant bits (MSbs) of the address are used to identify the location. Both the NuBus and VME (Versa Module European) buses, to only name a couple, use this type of addressing. Such an approach simplifies design by splitting the addressing space by number of connectors.

Borrill (1988) provides another approach to classing protocols than the standard synchronous–asynchronous dichotomy. He suggests three criteria, which are localization of the information validation (the locus), periodicity and flow control. The locus determines who has responsibility for the validation, whether it is the source (source-controlled), the destination (destination-controlled) or whether it is centralized. The periodicity states whether the exchange is periodic (fixed frequency) or aperiodic (variable frequency or synchronization). The control flow can be bounded (handshake) or not. On top of this, we can add the arbitration characteristics (*cf.* the following section).

1.6. Access arbitration

When there are simultaneously different access requests made to a bus, interruption requests (*cf.* Chapter V4-5), or Direct Memory Access (DMA, *cf.* § 2.2.2) requests made by a master or a slave (only for the first two), access arbitration to the bus is necessary. This involves choosing a master among n and allowing it to take the bus (grant). Access to the resource is exclusive. The electronics of the bus must be adapted in terms of output stages in order to (dis)connect to the arbiter request in a three-state logic, either open-collector or open-drain logic, or open-emitter or open source logic, depending on the technology used (*cf.* § 2.2.1 and 2.3 in Darche (2004)). In the case of a bidirectional bus, the direction of the flow of information must be invertible on command. Once the exchange has terminated, or under the constraint, the entity may release the bus. The arbiter is usually defined by a property of fairness of access. This means that it provides an identical service for all requesters, thus avoiding situations where the requester with the highest priority always gets access to the bus in the case of multiple requests. It also allows a requester with low priority to obtain access to the bus even when there are a large number of requests. This fairness can be weak, strong weighted or strong not weighted, or FIFO (First-In First-Out resource handling). An example of strong fairness is the matrix arbiter, which operates along a *last recently served* policy. An SP (Static Priority) arbitration is a predetermined allocation of the bus. This means that the bus can be allocated to nodes that have not requested access. Allocation can be determined by the bus cabling, that is, by the position of the node in the bus, or by software through programming. This simple solution is only suitable for a small number of nodes. Otherwise, arbitration has to be carried out as a function of the requesters, and is therefore dynamic (Dynamic Priority, DP).

The arbitration criteria are the location of the arbitration, the type of access request, allocation rules and bus release rules, the type of grant and the temporal relations between the arbitration and the transfer of data. The grant is valid for one or a given number of cycles, until the requester releases the bus, or on demand (preemption). With regard to localization, this can be centralized or distributed (the arbiter is decentralized), depending on the decision site. Thus, depending on the technique chosen, the arbitration electronics will be partially or completely located in the interface of the bus (*cf.* § 3.1), with the distributed version usually requiring more electronics. It is important to note that signaling can be synchronous or asynchronous[15] depending on the bus. Regarding the second point, allocation can be carried out either classically according to a fixed priority (it is prioritized), or it can be variable, a Round Robin (RR), for example. It can be sequential, that is, First-Come, First-Served (FCFS), also called FIFO, or democratic (no rules) (Bell 1978). Depending on the material solution chosen, not all of these can be implemented.

15 Plummer (1972) explores asynchronous arbiters, and Cowan and Whitehead (1976) presents a version with polling.

Priority can be set with cabling or through a program. An RR policy is easy to implemented. One disadvantage, however, is that a priority transfer (i.e. a quick one) cannot be granted as all those waiting must first be resolved. A TDMA (Time-Division Multiple-Access) policy allocates time slots (or time frames) that are either fixed or variable, and which guarantees the bandwidth and ensures that each is served. Dynamic reconfiguration allows the bandwidth requirements to be adapted to the bus. These are both single-level schemes. In order to improve the response time and bandwidth of the bus, a multi-level scheme can be used. One example is a TDMA/RR policy, which frees up an unused time slot that can then be allocated following an RR policy. Sonics SMART Interconnect is a bus that applies this scheme.

The three phases are demand, arbitration (also called resolution) and grant. Another way to describe the bus protocol is to use a Finite-State Machine (FSM, *cf.* § 3.7.3 in Darche (2002)). Its behavior can be described graphically using a state diagram like the one shown in Figure 1.35. Each circle represents a state, and the transition from one state to another takes place under the conditions specified by the arrows. If there is at least one request, the bus goes from the state of resolution to the state of addressing.

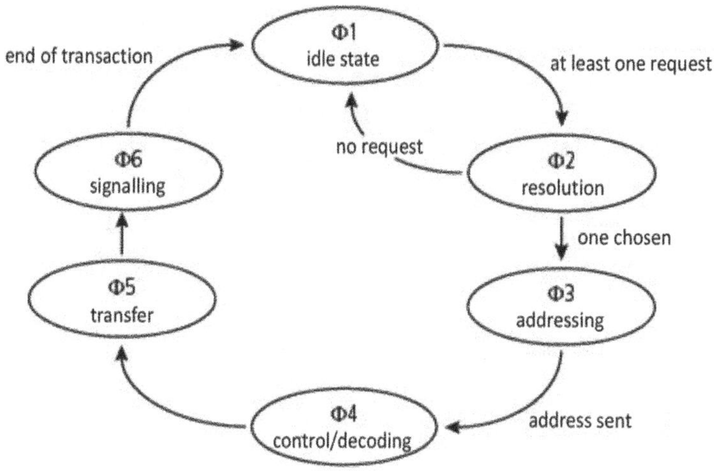

Figure 1.35. *Simplified state diagram of a bus protocol*

These three phases result in implementation through the following signals: Bus Request (BReq), Bus Grant (BG) and potentially a Bus Busy (BBusy) signal, or even a preemption request (Bus preempt) to remove the bus from the current holder. These are active at the low or high state depending on the implementation and technology of the logic used. These signals can circulate serially or in parallel between the nodes. A distinction can be made between several connection topologies. These are the daisy chain, the star, the bus or a mixed solution drawing on the best aspects of the different approaches. The three most common communication diagrams for receiving requests or sending out arbitration responses are the daisy chain, independent requests and polling.

The daisy chain is a type of link between communicating nodes, each with an input signal and an output signal, thus creating a chain between them. This signal can be the access grant to a bus, as is the case in Figure 1.36. This daisy chain allows for a serial distributed arbitration solution to be reached. It is distributed as each node is in possession of its own arbiter. The requests are made in parallel thanks to a wired OR. A node that wants the bus activates the request line if its BPRI (Bus PRiority In) input is not active. The other nodes propagate the request up to the requesting node, which then becomes the bus owner, while maintaining its request. Resolution is therefore conducted serially. The bus state can be read in the BPRI input. In principle, allocation is fixed by the geographical position of the nodes in the loop, and is therefore not fair. This is a simple and cheap solution, as it does not involve a lot of logic (Figure 1.40). However, it is slow because the response has to go from node to node. Another disadvantage is the complex cabling, as, for example, in the case of a backplane bus with slottable daughter cards, the continuity of the chain must be maintained. This can be done using a strap, or with a dummy board, a bit like what is done in the CRIMM[16] module (Continuity Rambus In-line Memory Module, *cf.* § 7.2.1 in Darche (2012)). Moreover, if one of the nodes fails, some of the nodes are then isolated and therefore become blocked. A daisy chain model is studied in exercise E1.4.

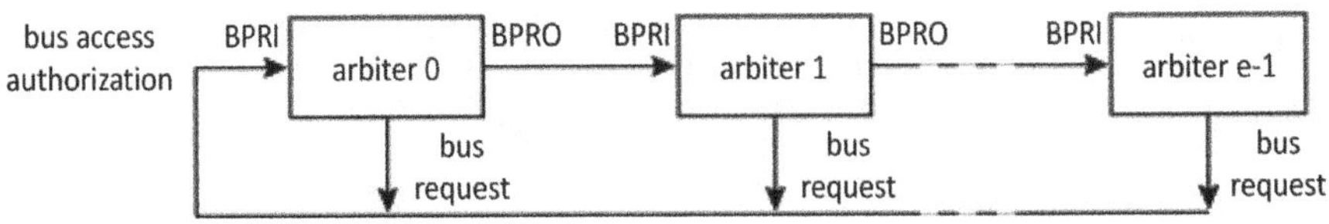

Figure 1.36. *Another version of daisy chain distributed arbitration (from Thurber et al. (1972))*

Figure 1.37 presents a variation on the previous version, this time with a permanent state of grant for taking the bus for the first arbiter (no. 0). If it wants the

16 This type of link was already covered for I/O (*cf.* § 1.2.3 in Darche (2003)) and for memory (*cf.* § 5.3 in Darche (2012)).

bus, and if the bus is free, it takes the bus and activates the corresponding state line. If the bus is busy, it waits for it to become free. If it does not want it, it activates its BPRO (Bus PRiority Out) output, passing its right of access to the next one along the chain.

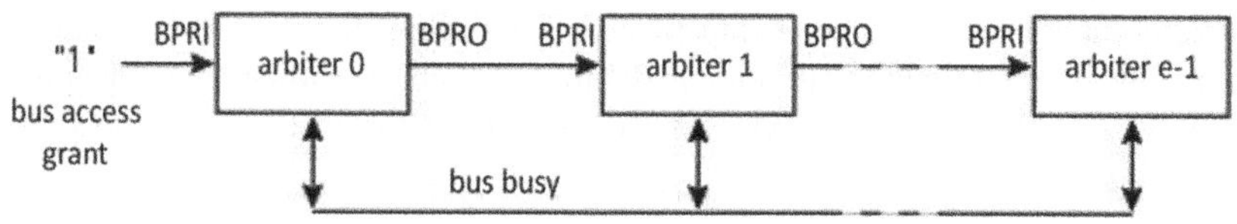

Figure 1.37. *Daisy chain arbitration (variation)*

Figure 1.38 shows a simpler version of this, but the state of the bus cannot be determined on a grant signal level, but rather on an edge.

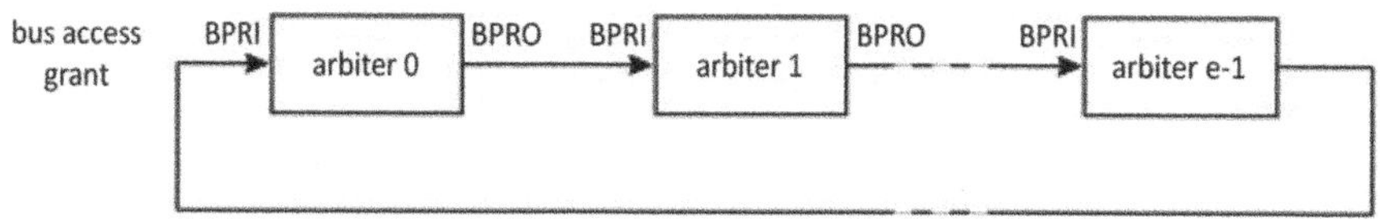

Figure 1.38. *A simple solution for daisy chain distributed arbitration (from Thurber et al. (1972))*

Figure 1.39 shows a centralized version. Requests are made in parallel. An access grant is given by the controller, but priority is fixed by the physical cabling of the nodes with the same weaknesses as before, which concern priority and tolerance to material faults. The entity that takes the bus and keeps the bus signals to it through the occupation line. It should be noted that if this line is removed, we revert to the daisy chain solution from Figure 1.36. Several loops or request-grant chain levels can exist in order to create a priority hierarchy (multi-level arbiter). Exercise E1.3 is an example of a study in parallel arbiters.

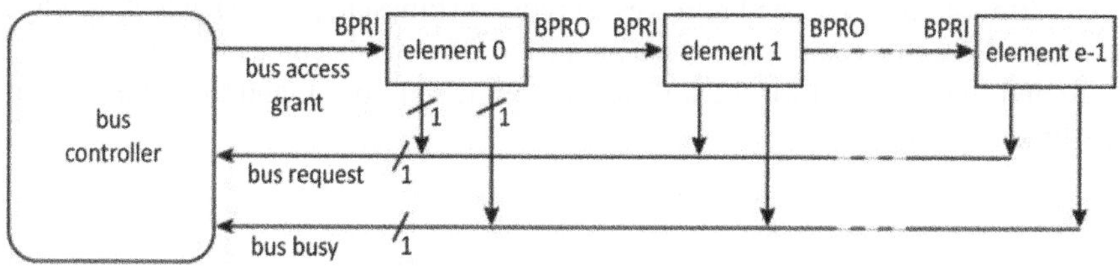

Figure 1.39. *Centralized version of the daisy chain*

Figure 1.40 describes the control logic at the level of each node, which blocks agreement according to priorities linked to the geographical position of the element within the bus. Spatial priority can be changed thanks to specific cabling using cavaliers or straps, as described in Borrill (1981), although this is a very onerous solution to put in place, and can result in mechanical faults. Inverters have an output that is compatible with them being placed in parallel, that is, a collector or open drain, for example. The simplicity of the flowchart should not disguise the complexity of the timescales, which need to account for all the bus delays and the processing electronics.

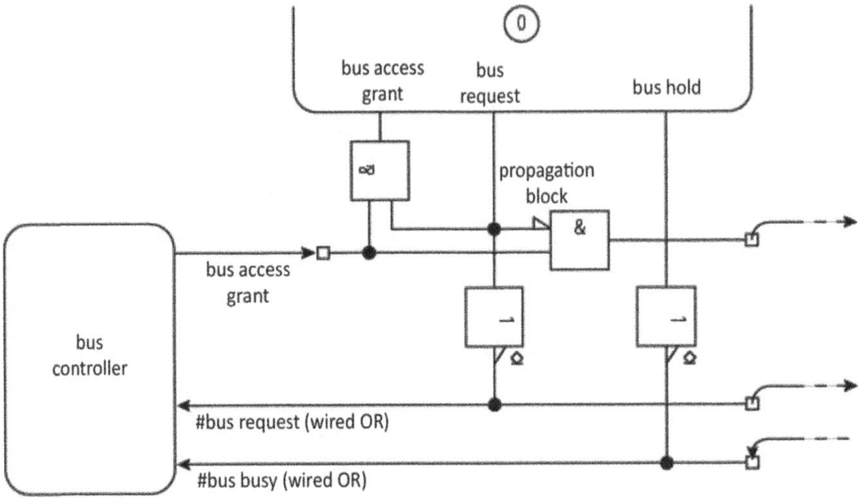

Figure 1.40. *Daisy chain agreement bus access control logic (simplified)*

The preceding example was inspired by the Unibus™ bus from the PDP-11 made by the company DEC. Figure 1.41 presents the corresponding process chronograms (positive logic). A node requests access (timestamp no. 1). Access is granted to the first node concerned (timestamp no. 2). This node acknowledges receipt (timestamp no. 3) and removes its request (timestamp no. 4), which results in the grant also being removed (timestamp no. 5). The bus becomes free (time interval no. 6) and then blocked for the transfer (time interval no. 7), and the arbiter signals this (time interval no. 8).

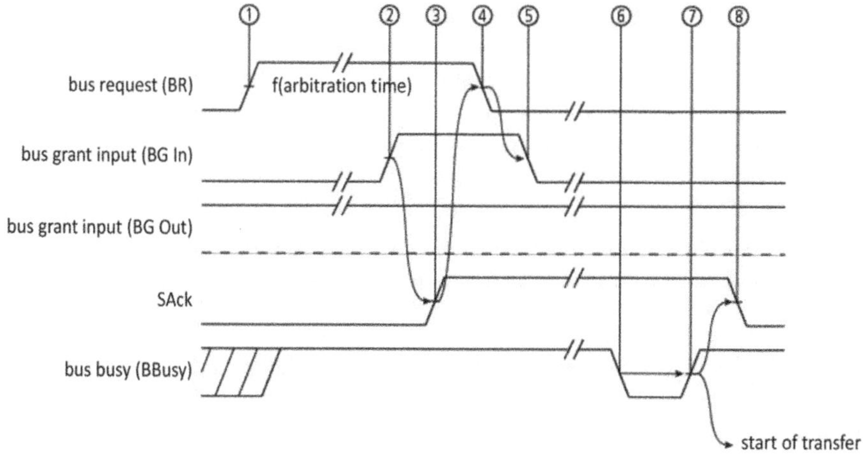

Figure 1.41. *Unibus™ bus arbitration sequence*

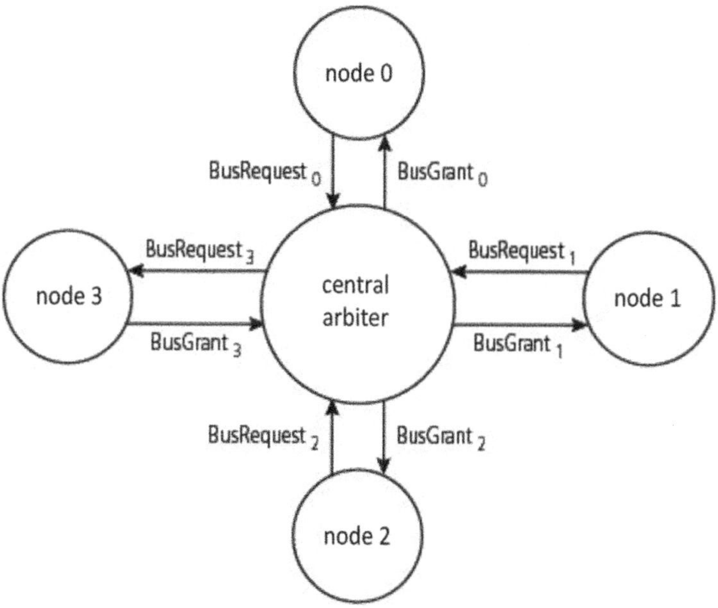

Figure 1.42. *Topology of a centralized arbitration*

In order to get around the major inconvenience of a chain break, an independent request approach can be used. Figure 1.43 presents a centralized version inspired by bus PCI (PCI-SIG 1998). Each request and each grant are independent of each other. They are carried out in an asynchronous manner. For this, the arbiter, or manager, must be highlighted within the bus controller as the one that receives requests and, depending on the access policies, determines which entities can get access to the bus. Examples among the commercial arbiters are the 74xxx148, 74F786 and 82C89 (by Intel). In the example shown in Figure 1.42, a couple of signals ($request_i$, $grant_i$) handle access to the bus. A requesting node i (i ∈ [0, 3]) generates its access request to the bus Req_i (*Bus Request*) and receives its grant Grt_i (*Bus PRiority iN*, sometimes called BPRN).

A priority encoder (Figure 1.43) establishes the number of the line to be served according to a given policy. The request and resolution are in parallel here. Arbitration of the VME bus is carried out in this way for n = 2, that is, for four lines of authorization request. Centralized arbitration is simple to execute, but the number of nodes is limited. The bus manager always needs to know whether there is a request currently underway, and whether the bus is busy or released, which depends on the shared signal of bus busy CBusy (for Common Busy), which is not shown. In order to avoid a shortage in the case where a node does not release the bus and another with higher priority asks for it, the bus manager can order the immediate release of the bus by deactivating its grant.

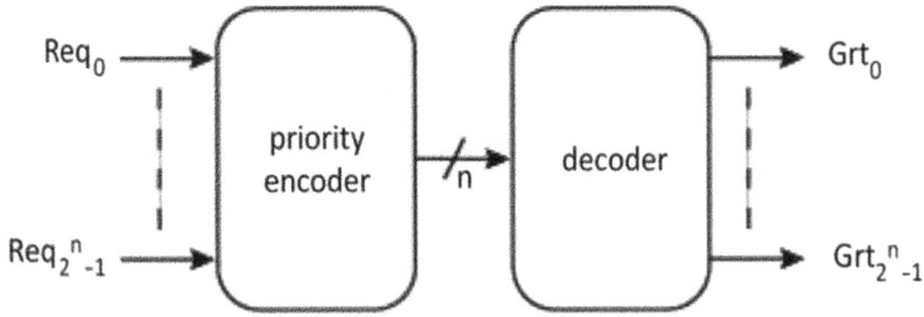

Figure 1.43. *Centralized arbiter with independent request and resolution*

The sequence diagram in Figure 1.44 provides an example of centralized arbitration with fixed priorities. Node no. 0 has the highest priority. The bus is free. Node no. 1 requests the bus, and is then granted permission to take it. It takes the bus, then frees it. Node no. 0 does the same. While this last node is master of the bus, node no. 1 makes a request that will always be denied while a higher-priority node (in this case, node no. 0) is in possession of the bus. When the bus has been freed, it can then take it. We can see here that fixed priority is not fair.

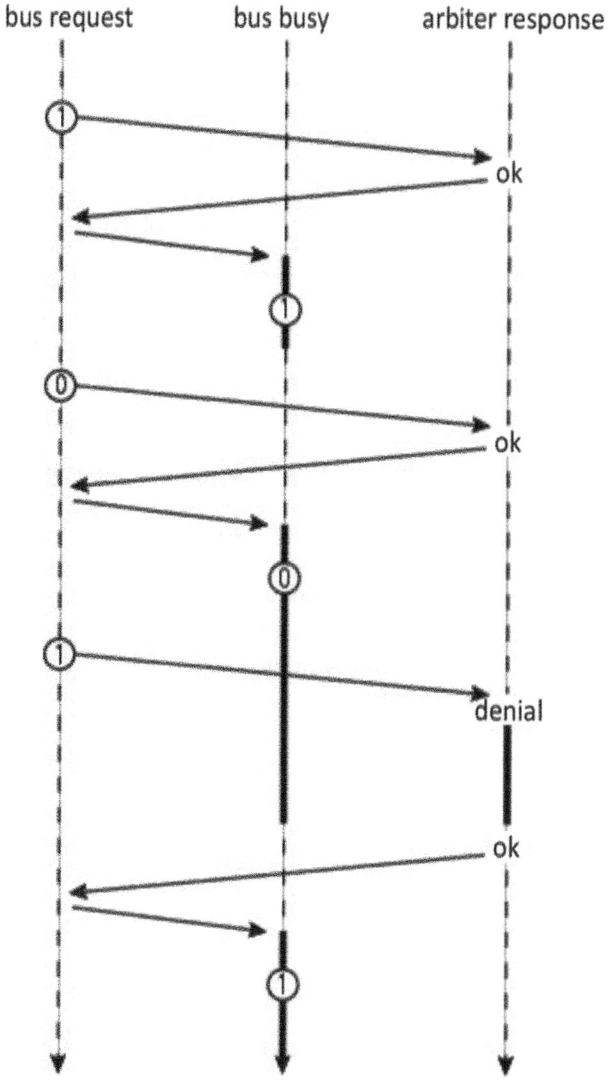

Figure 1.44. *Example of a centralized arbitration protocol with a daisy chain response*

Figure 1.45 shows the distributed version of a solution with independent requests. The requesters place their priorities along one of the lines of the request bus. This is an expensive option in terms of the width of the bus, but it is easy to set up in terms of electronics. The node in current possession of the bus deactivates the "bus assigned" signal; the node with the highest priority can then acquire possession of the bus by activating the assignment signal.

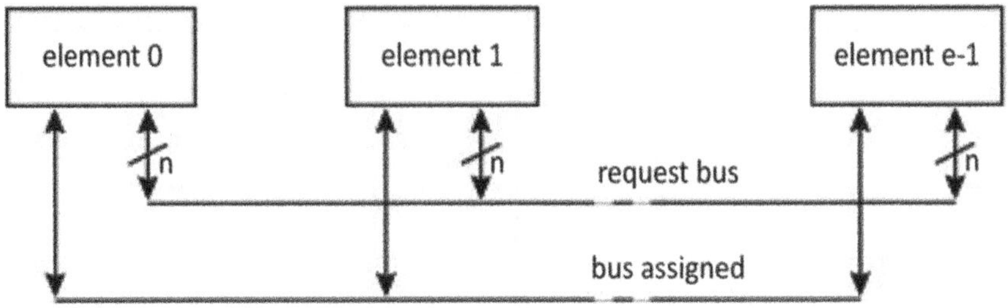

Figure 1.45. *Arbitration by independent requests in a decentralized version*

Polling is another option that involves cyclically questioning nodes in order to establish which is the requester (Figure 1.46). The node with the number corresponding to the current value of the counter activates the occupation line, which causes the counting to stop. Once the bus has been freed, if an access request has been made, the counter can start a poll again, either by restarting the counter or by starting again from the last node that has been granted access. The second option has the advantage of providing rotating priority, while the former provides the same as there would be in a daisy chain.

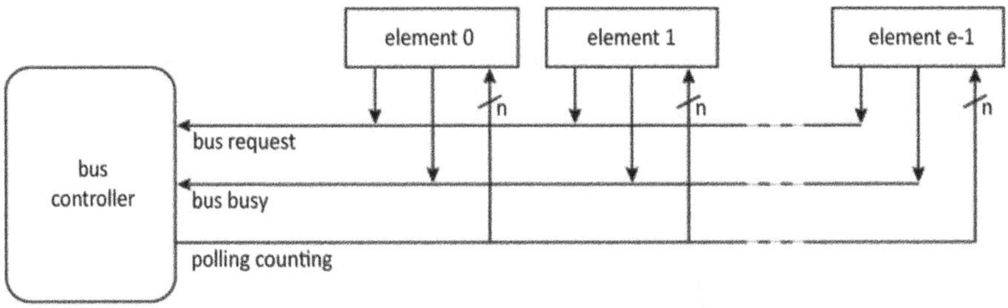

Figure 1.46. *Centralized arbitration by polling (from Thurber et al. (1972))*

In order to remove the request line, the counting is decentralized and a global clock signal Clk paces the counting (Figure 1.47). If a node wants the bus and the value of its counter is equal to its number, then it activates the occupation line, which results in the counting stopping. As before, after the bus is released, the counting can either return to its current value or be restarted depending on the priority policy desired. This type of mechanism is sensitive to noise.

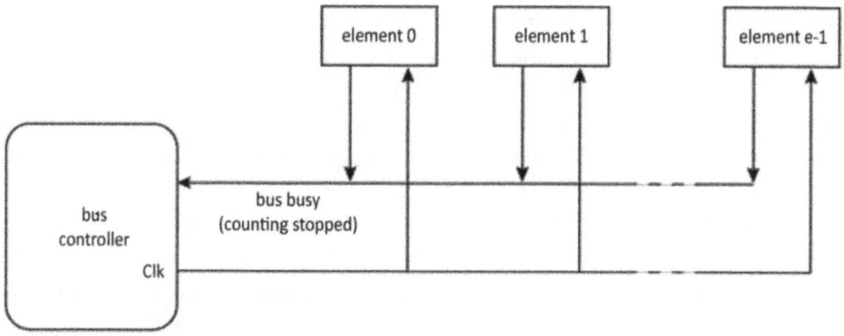

Figure 1.47. *Centralized arbitration by polling*

When a node frees the bus in a distributed version (Figure 1.48), it positions the "bus free" signal and a number on the polling bus. This can represent an address or a priority. If this value corresponds to a node, the node in question activates the acceptance signal, which results in the "bus free" signal being deactivated. If this is not the case, however, counting takes place indefinitely according to the chosen priority policy until a positive response is received from one of the nodes.

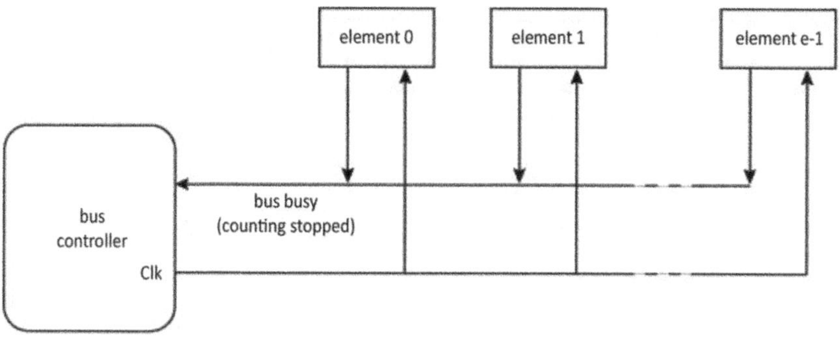

Figure 1.48. *Distributed arbitration by polling*

In a distributed self-selection approach, each entity is an agent in the negotiation. There is a linear version (with a linear self-selection arbiter), which has as many lines as nodes, but the number of which can be reduced with coded version (this is a coded self-selection arbiter). Here, we have an example of distributed arbitration, inspired by buses MCA (*Micro Channel Architecture*), S-100 (IEEE Std 696 (ANSI/IEEE 1982b)), FASTBUS (IEEE 1989) or Futurebus (IEEE Std 896 (IEEE 1994)). Access to the buses is provided synchronously (by cycle). The arbitration phases are the following: at the start of a cycle, the interested units emit the value of their priority over the bus (excluding values of zero). The address thus formed is the "logical OR" of the addresses thanks to outputs like the collector or the open drain (*cf.* § 2.2.1 and 2.3 in Darche (2004)). The absorbing element is therefore the value "1" when the outputs are not active. During the arbitration cycle, the units listen to the bus and change their emission to 0 (i.e. they deactivate its lines) for bits with a weight that is less than the position of the first difference (the order is MSb → LSb for Least Significant bit). The winner is the unit that recognizes the value of its priority on the bus. Figure 1.49 shows a real example of this. A major disadvantage is that the priority is fixed and therefore not fair. Kipnis (1989) formalized the protocol, and Taub (1984) describes the arbitration diagram of the Futurebus.

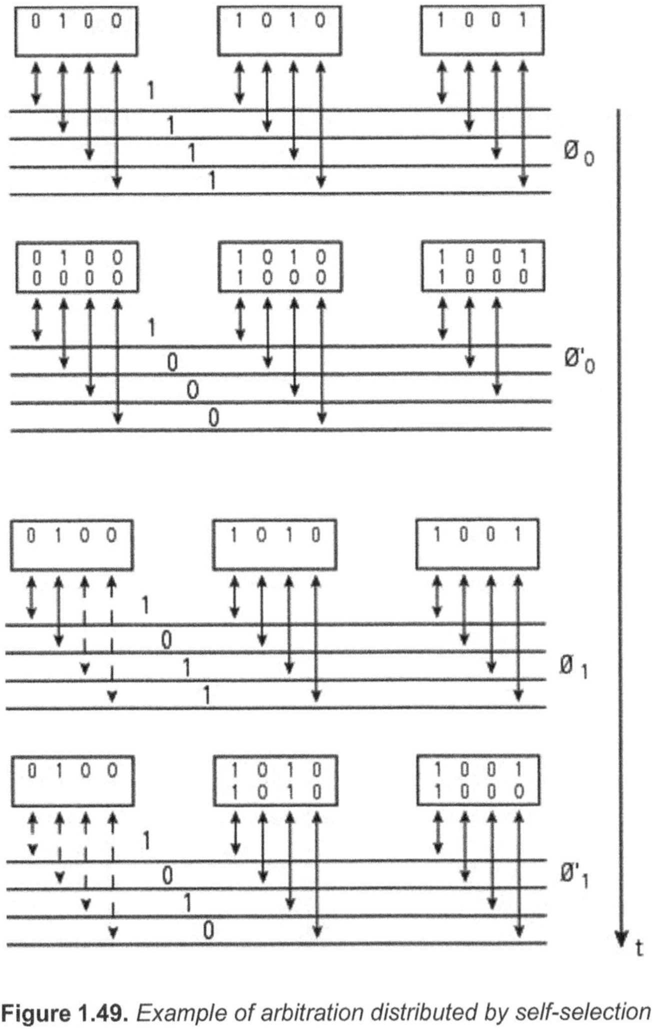

Figure 1.49. *Example of arbitration distributed by self-selection*

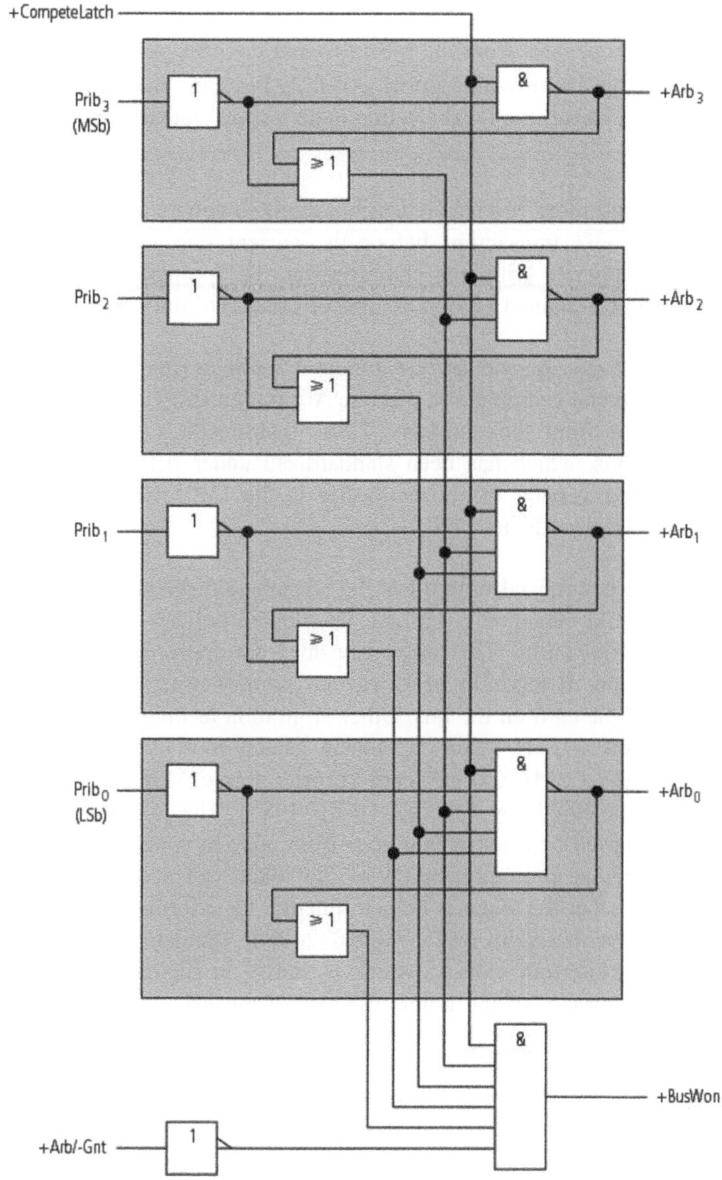

Figure 1.50. *Local arbiter from the MCA bus*

Figure 1.50 provides an example of the local arbiter logic, in this case from the MCA bus. A central arbiter is tasked with managing the arbitration phase by authorizing the local arbitration phase and detecting when it has ended. The arbitration serially propagates from the MSb towards the LSb. As soon as a stage i ($i \in [0, 3]$) detects that its bit with a priority of $Prib_i$ is greater than the one present on the bus ($+Arb_i$), it causes the local election to be lost by blocking the lower AND gates.

Overlapping arbitration (anticipated arbitration) involves carrying out the arbitration for the next transaction before the current one has finished. Both Unibus™ and PCI operate with this characteristic. The property of bus parking allows possession to be retained as long as another master has not yet requested it.

Bus arbitration logic is one of the function modules of the bus interface (*cf.* § 3.1). A commercial example of a discrete Arbitration Bus Controller (ABC) is the TFB2010 circuit from the company Texas Instruments (TI), made for the Futurebus+ (FB+) bus, which has been standardized under IEEE Std 896 (IEEE 1994). An integrated version of the controller is the MPU NS32132 from the company National Semiconductor (NS).

In summary, the centralized option has the advantage of being simpler, but the number of nodes to be managed is limited. Distributed policies are more tolerant with regard to material faults. This obviously does not apply to the daisy chain, which is an exception. It tends to be slow, and priority usually depends on the physical position of the card on the bus. Other arbitration techniques do exist, such as collision detection and ID tokens. Collision detection is used in the field of networks through the CSMA/CD protocol (Carrier Sense Multiple Access with Collision Detection method) by Ethernet (IEEE 1985). The use of ID tokens is another technique, based on a token that goes from node to node (sequential token passing). The node that is in possession of the token can access the bus. The protocol must ensure that the token is unique. Finally, for informative purposes, the main arbitration protocols are covered in Guibaly (1989). Dandamudi (2003) created a classification of arbitration criteria, which is shown in Figures 1.51 and 1.52, which are perfect summary of the points we have made heretofore. The first one covers organization, allocation policies and bus release.

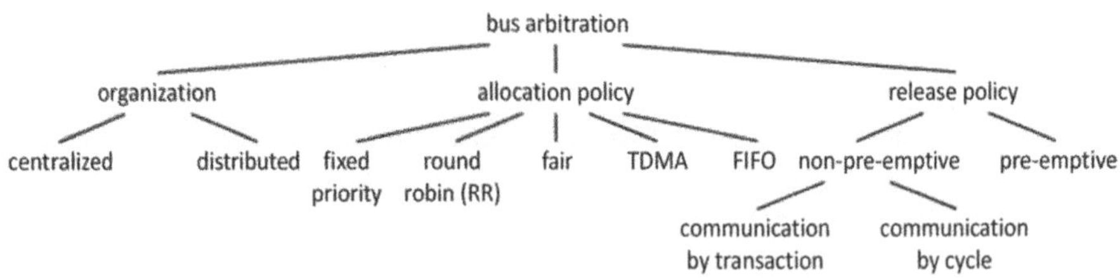

Figure 1.51. *Design tree of a bus arbitration*

The second figure classes the access requests and grants.

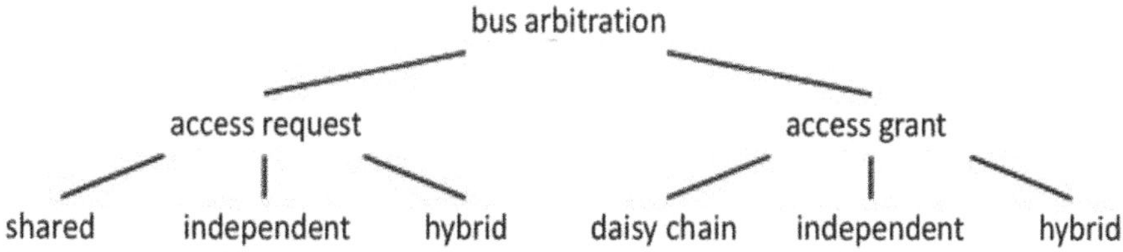

Figure 1.52. *Design tree of a bus arbitration (continued and end)*

1.7. Conclusion

After some general points regarding communication, the main mechanical, electrical and temporal characteristics of buses were presented. These can potentially be specified within a reference standard, which would allow for further standardization of electronic and mechanical components, thus reducing costs. Next, we looked at the notions of protocol and arbitration. Exchange by the synchronous approach was examined in great detail.

2

Transactions and Special Cycles

This chapter focuses on transactions. These are important as they provide a solution to the bottleneck problem. In this context, we shall cover the following modes of transfer: pipelined, split and Out-of-Order (OoO, an extension of the split mode). Moreover, in addition to the classical cycles of read and write, this chapter also covers cycles that are termed "special", such as broadcasting and block transfers.

2.1. Transaction

A transaction is made up of a sequence of messages. A message is the base unit of any information. It comprises an address, data and an access type. The three phases of a bus cycle are access request (usually in a multi-master environment), addressing and data transfer. There is also sometimes a termination phase. The request itself is split into a request, an arbitration and a grant of possession of the bus.

2.1.1. *Transaction pipeline*

All of the (sub)phases of a transaction that are normally carried out sequentially can also be executed in parallel if they are placed into the different functional stages of a pipeline. This is called a pipelined bus, with a pipelined transaction. This approach involves functionally splitting the transaction into sub-steps in order to execute them in parallel in the same number of stages. This is used in Synchronous Static and Dynamic Random Access Memory (SSRAM and SDRAM, *cf.* § 4.5.1 and 6.1 in Darche (2012)). Figure 2.1 shows how a write operation can be split into phases. The request involves sending the address and type of transfer requested. The transfer, address and data phases are overlaid onto each other.

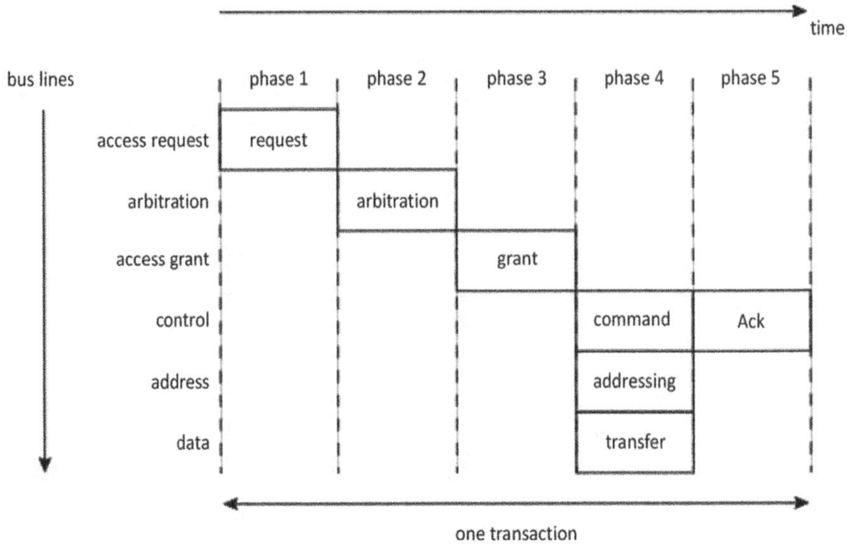

Figure 2.1. *Pipelined write operation split into phases*

For a read to be carried out in phases, a wait cycle has to take place in order for the read to be effective. This is shown in gray in Figure 2.2.

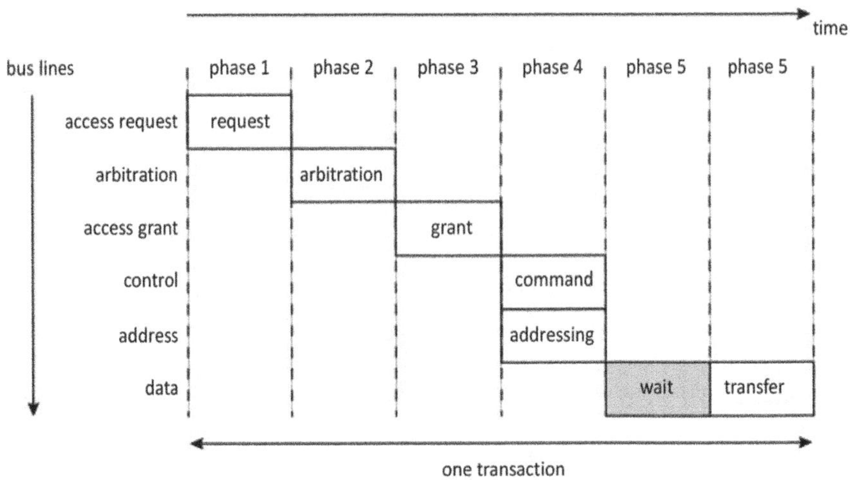

Figure 2.2. *Pipelined read operation split into phases*

The point of this functional splitting is that it opens up the possibility of introducing partial parallel operating, as shown in Figure 2.3. This notably frees up time for decoding the addresses.

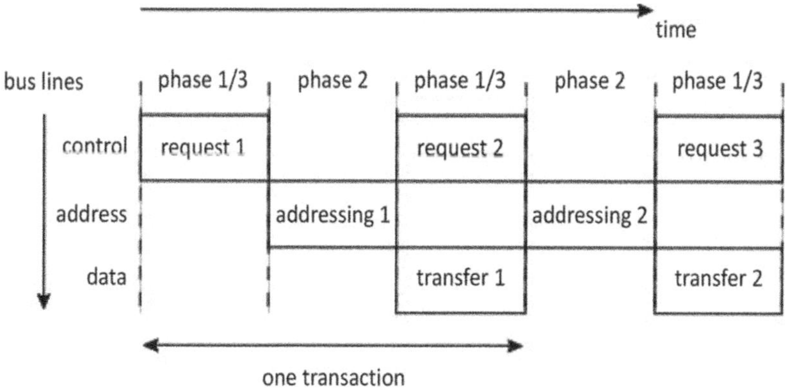

Figure 2.3. *Transactions with partially parallel phases*

Maximization of this parallelism results in transfer pipelining, as illustrated in Figure 2.4. The address of the next transaction is sent in advance to the dedicated bus before the current transaction has ended. After a certain structure loading time has passed, the pipeline is fully effective, and the data bus is 100% occupied. In the example, this occurs from the third request onward. The transfer of data requested during previous phases takes place in parallel to any new requests.

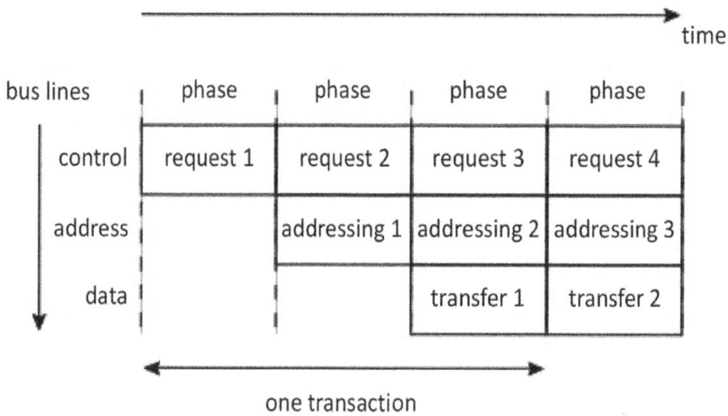

Figure 2.4. *Pipelined transactions*

Sometimes, it becomes necessary to temporarily stop the progress of the request along the pipeline for the duration of one clock cycle because of a conflict of access in the bus. This forced wait time is called a "stall cycle" and is shown in Figure 2.5. One of the operating rules is there can only ever be one slave in possession of the bus at any time. Another rule is that a grant can be made when the bus is being used, but not until it has been freed by the current owner.

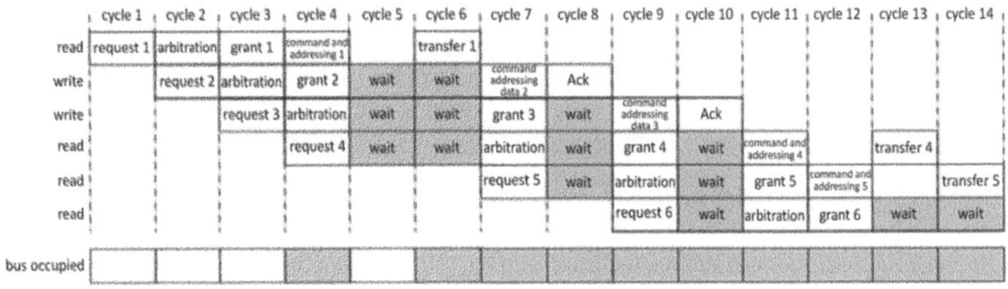

Figure 2.5. *Stall cycles in a pipeline*

2.1.2. *Splitting the transaction*

In the previous subsection, we have just seen that, in a pipeline, an increase in the number of functional stages results in an increase in bit-rate, but strict sequencing causes stalls, which lower the bit-rates of the buses (*cf.* above). Competition in terms of access can be introduced by splitting the transaction into two separate sub-transactions, which are the request transaction and the reply transaction. This is illustrated in Figure 2.6. In this way, while awaiting the response, the bus can be released for another access request and then given away again in order to finish off the first transaction. This is what is known as a split transaction. The associated bus is called a split-phase or packet-switched bus. The address and data phases are completely separate from each other, as is their arbitration. For this reason, they share a tag, which is generated during the first phase, which must subsequently correspond to the tag from the second phase.

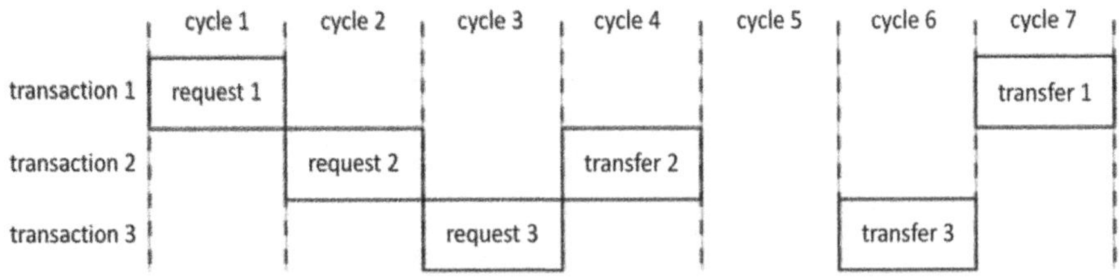

Figure 2.6. *Split transaction*

The order in which the address bus, followed by the data bus, are taken is maintained (classical pipeline). However, extension of the splitting allows for an out-of-order processing, as takes place in microprocessors. This means that the order of the transfers does not have to follow the order of the requests, as shown in Figure 2.6, where transfer 1 takes place after transfers 2 and 3. This allows for further optimization of how the bus space is occupied. A commercial example is the PowerPath-2™ bus from the Challenge family (Galles and Williams 1994) made by SGI (Silicon Graphics, Inc.). To order transactions, this bus has to connect the request and the transfer. To do this, it uses a tag with a format of n = 3 bits, which enables it to link them together rather than to the address. Another commercial example is the Gigaplane™ bus from the company Sun. The exchange can be synchronous or not.

In order to respect real-time constraints, preemption can be added to this approach, which allows the bus controller to take the bus away from an entity with lower priority, and allocate it to one with higher priority (this is transaction preemption). The interrupted transaction can be resumed later on (transaction resumption). Lastly, overlapping arbitration (*cf.* § 1.6) enables overlapping address and data phases to be carried out.

2.2. Special cycles

Beyond the classic transfers of read and write, there are also other types of access, such as read–modify–write, diffusion and broadcall. The first of these was explained in the context of dynamic random access memory (DRAM, *cf.* § 5.2.1 in Darche (2012)). In a single cycle, it can read and then write a single piece of data in the same location. This function can be used in the case of a critical section for changing an access lock. Broadcast allows a master to write an element of data in various different slaves in the same cycle. One use of this is to maintain coherence in several caches. Broadcall is a read operation where several slaves position information on the bus. This can be used in the detection of several interrupt requests coming from various sources, by carrying out wired AND or OR functions (*cf.* § 4.1.1 in Darche (2003)). These two types of transfer can be contrasted with an addressed transfer.

There are two fundamental types of transfer, either unique by word and multiple by block of varying or fixed lengths (these are block-oriented transactions), or block-word combinations of fixed or varying lengths. During a simple cycle, for example, for a read operation, after any possible arbitration has been conducted, a command and an address are sent to transfer one word after each cycle. In order to increase the rate of memories sent, and to adapt to the transfer mode of the cache memory, a block transfer mode can be used. It resembles the burst mode of RAM (*cf.* § 5.5.2 and 4.4.5 in Darche (2012), and also the chapters on SDRAM (no. 6) and on memories using packet-based communication (no. 7) in the same work). This allows for the consecutive block transfer of n words from the memory (*cf.* § 4.4.5 and 6.3 in Darche (2012)). Only the address at the start of the block being transferred circulates along the bus, and potentially the number of words to transfer, if this is not clear, as well as the data (Figure 2.7). A burst mode is greater than the value of the unit flow multiplied by the size of the block. It is equally adapted to Input/Output (I/O) transactions. This approach is better when used with a multiplexed address/data bus. However, requests coming from other nodes must also be considered, especially those with real-time constraints. One solution to this is to limit the length of the bursts, or to add preemption, which interrupts the transaction and allows it to be continued later.

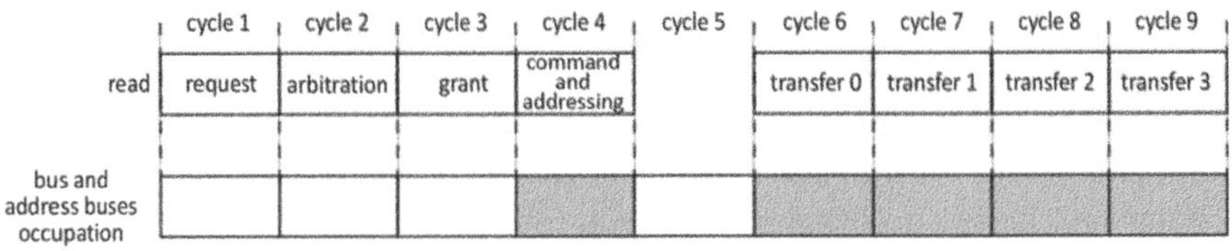

Figure 2.7. *Read by block*

Lastly, there are also other transfer modes. An example is the address-only modes, without any data, which can be used for a dialogue with the cache, for example. Others are the TLB (Translation Lookaside Buffer, *cf.* V2 on future memory devices), compelled-data, or packet-data. In a compelled-data mode, the slave has to provide a response before the master can move on to another transfer (IEEE 1991).

2.2.1. *Managing interruption*

The mechanics behind interruption is of importance not only to the management of I/O, but also in the handling of errors and, especially, for Operating System (OS) calls. There are two types of interruption, which depend on the origin of the request, which can be either software or hardware (*cf.* the classification in § 4.1.1 in Darche (2003) and § V4-5.1). The latter is the one of interest here, and in this case, these are the specific input signals of the microprocessor. Each input is sensitive to a single level or transition of the signal. The request lines can be unique to each slave S, or the request can be shared. In this case, outputs of the L(ow) type must be used, which correspond to the collector of an NPN transistor, or the open drain of a PMOS (Positive (channel) Metal Oxide Semiconductor, *cf.* § 2.1.3 in Darche (2004)), depending on the logic technology used (Figure 2.8).

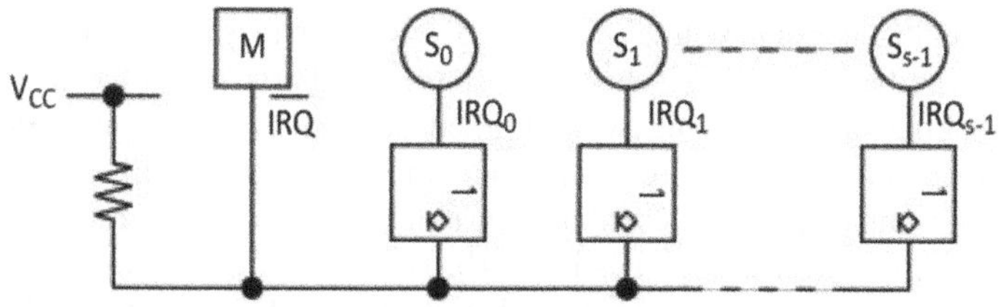

Figure 2.8. *Interruption bus*

Figure 2.9 shows an electric circuit corresponding to the outputs of the open drain or open collector types. These parallel electronic interrupts connect the request line to the ground, forming a wired negative logic OR function and a wired positive logic AND function (*cf.* § 3.4.5 in Darche (2004)). The sharing of interrupt requests is a possibility here, as long as the request is level-sensitive at the level of the master, as opposed to being carried out by transition, which would result in any requests coming after the first one not being detected. For this reason, the extension bus ISA[1] (Industry Standard Architecture, *cf.* § 4.2.4) could not share an interrupt request line. This problem can be overcome using a software solution, and by setting up a polling technique. However, this solution has its own intrinsic limitations (i.e. risk of loss of request and high computing power requirements.

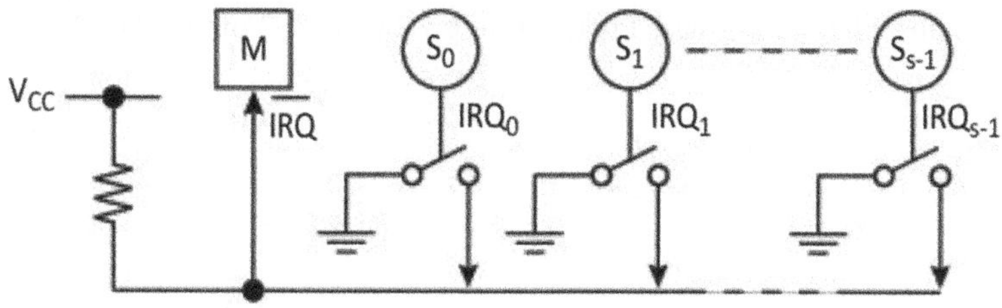

Figure 2.9. *Interrupt bus*

Each request line or interrupt number is associated with an interrupt handler. In order to start it, first its start address must be known. This is called the interrupt vector. This vector is typically stored in a table called the interrupt vector table (*cf.* § V4-5.7), which is itself saved in the main memory. During a bus cycle, the interrupt phase corresponds to the transfer of the interrupt vector toward the processor processing the request. For this to happen, the origin of the requests – whether of bus access, interrupt, DMA transfer (*cf.* next §), by slave or by master – must first be determined physically. This can be achieved using a daisy chain, which

1 Not to be confused with the ISA (Instruction Set Architecture, *cf.* § V1-3.5).

passes the dialogue grant with the master from slave to slave. This technique is called "proximity addressing". For the closest authorized entity, this dialogue involves making an identifying word (called vector) available on the bus. This vector corresponds to the address, whether direct or indirect, of the start of the corresponding interrupt handler. Another solution is to activate the bus lines associated with the slave being questioned (broad-collect cycle) (Nicoud 1987). The mechanism behind interrupts is explained in detail in Chapter V4-5 and for I/O in § 4.1.1 of Darche (2003).

2.2.2. *Managing direct memory access*

We saw in Chapter 1 of Darche (2003) that any information coming from the memory from the I/O should in principle pass through the registers of the MPU (MicroProcessor Unit). Direct memory access (DMA) is a mechanism that allows the processor to be relieved of this transfer, which is a role taken on by a specialized controller (Figure 2.10). The processor programs (i.e. initiates) the DMA Controller (DMAC) by telling it what the source and destination addresses are, as well as the number of memory words to transfer. It then starts the transaction. The buses are shared between two masters: processor P, which is free to take on another activity, and the DMAC, which carries out the transaction. The microprocessor is warned of the end of the transaction through a general interrupt (*cf.* § 2.2.1 and Chapter V4-5). This mechanism has been studied in detail in § 1.2 and 4.1.3 of Darche (2003).

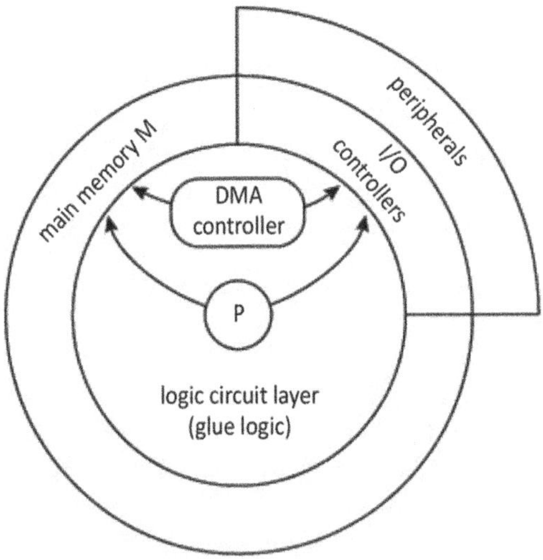

Figure 2.10. *Exchanges between the main memory and classical I/O units and by direct memory access*

2.2.3. *Bus Mastering*

Bus Mastering (BM) allows a bus expansion card to take control of the bus through the arbiter (Integrated System Peripheral (ISP) chip). Reference circuit 82367 by Intel is representative of this concept. The expansion buses (*cf.* § 4.5) EISA (Extended ISA) and PCI contain this function. It is different from classical DMA ("third[2] party" DMA), in that it is not the MPU that initiates the transfer of the descriptor (source and destination addresses, and length), but rather one of the cards. One of the card's local DMA controllers is usually needed ("first party" or BM DMA). In order to avoid one card penalizing all the others, an order of priority is required. This normally has four levels, which are system memory refresh, the DMA transaction, the MPU transaction and the BM. One of the first interfaces to use this was the SCSI (Small Computer System Interface, *cf.* § 9.3.1 in Darche (2003) and Schmidt (1995)). The Ultra DMA transfer (UDMA, *cf.* § 4.1.3 in Darche (2003)) is another example for hard drive mass storage memory devices or HDD (Hard Disk Drive).

2.2.4. *Detection and correction of errors*

Packet communication helps to reduce errors, in both the absolute and metaphorical sense. Detection takes place at the level of the packet, which allows for easy and rapid rectification of the error. Classical examples of error detection and correction protocols that can be applied to packets are the Alternating-Bit (AB, also called the Stop-and-Wait) protocol and the Automatic Repeat reQuest (ARQ) protocols (Fairhurst and Wood 2002), which is a form of the sliding window protocol. These include the go-back-N technique (also called REJect technique or REJ) and the selective-repeat (also called Selective Reject, SREJ) technique. These are not covered in this work.

2.2.5. *Multiprocessor aspect*

In the 1980s, a multi-master bus would allow communication between a mono-processor system and co-processors or transaction facilitators, such as a DMA controller (DMAC). Nowadays, multi-master systems contain several processors that each have their own cache memory and main memory, and furthermore physically share a cache memory and a main memory. They therefore have a private address space (AS, *cf.* § V3-2.1.1.1) and, possibly, a shared AS as well. The interrupt request and DMA signals are hard to process in such an environment. The

---

2 The first two elements are the source and destination, respectively. The controller (the third party) handles the transfer.

bus has to be able to provide a range of options for the designer in terms of arbitration (centralized or distributed, different selection policies, maximum number of requests processed, etc.). Moreover, the current trend is to use an electrical signal to replace these interrupt requests and DMA transfer mechanisms with the mechanism used in the message passing, as shared memory communication is not suitable for this. The requests are then encapsulated within a classic data transfer so as to not specialize the bus signals for a given type of microprocessor, and so that it can easily adapt to the microprocessor environment.

2.3. Conclusion

The notion of transaction has allowed an access to be split into several sub-steps, which can then be put in parallelized thanks to a pipeline. Special cycles are solutions that help deal with mechanisms such as interruption and direct memory transfer. Bus mastering is a way of avoiding, always having to go through the MPU for any exchange. In order to make communication more reliable, mechanisms for detecting and correcting errors have been proposed, both in terms of software and in terms of hardware. The current trend is a shift toward serial buses and packet-based communication, thus moving away from the cycle.

3

Bus Interfaces

In order for connections to be made with a bus, each of its nodes must have an interface. This chapter covers the notions relating to these interfaces.

3.1. Functional modules

The nodes of a bus, which usually take on the physical form of an electronic board, can be modeled as two sub-sets (Figure 3.1): the user module and the bus interface (I/F). The user module can be a master M or a slave S. Examples of this are the MPU (MicroProcessor Unit), memory devices or Input–Output (I/O) controllers. The bus interface enables dialogue between the user module – whether master or slave – and the bus. It can be modeled functionally by two sub-sets which are the interfacing logic and management elements or functional modules.

For buses operating synchronously, a distinction must be made between the bus interface and the user module. If the state machine of the interface is paced by a clock, then it is called a "clocked interface". If the host is paced by another clock, or operates asynchronously, this can result in clock issues, such as metastability (*cf.* § 3.5.2 in Darche (2004)) due to the presence of two clock domains (CDC for "Clock Domain Crossing", *cf.* § 3.6.6 in Darche (2012)) and violation of the golden rule of access (i.e. bus-setup and hold times, *cf.* § 3.3.4 in Darche (2012)) that applies to the flip-flops. If both entities are paced by the same clock signal, this is called a "clocked protocol" (Corso *et al.* 1986).

Functional modules, or management elements, have historically controlled access to the bus (request, arbitration, grant, preemption), interruptions (request, ID vector, state) and DMA type transfers (Direct Memory Access, *cf.* § 2.2.2). Another function is the creation of bus timing signals. Lastly, address decoding helps select a slave that has to respond. The slave is activated by the address, potentially with a geographical form of addressing, such as the slot number (*cf.* § 1.5). There are several types of selection: decoded, coded or mixed; this depends on the position of the decoder in relation to the inside or the outside of the slave. Moreover, incomplete decoding can be chosen in order to cut costs, which results in ghost addresses (*cf.* § 2.2.2 in Darche (2003)). Nowadays, the current can be finely managed in order to control the power-on and power-off processes of the user and to regulate system current use or the hot swapping of electronic boards. Examples include the conversion of bus protocols and the temporary storage of information through FIFO (First-In, First-Out) resource handling, thus adapting the bitrate between the bus and the nodes (*cf.* V2 on semi-conductor memory devices). Lastly, the board can possess a ROM (Read-Only Memory) containing a piece of firmware (FW) for setup, startup and handling of the I/O (extra BIOS (Basic Input/Output System, *cf.* § V5-3.5.3)), or even pre-saved management parameters if the memory device is programmable. Setup can involve defining an address or a whole range of addresses. A network interface can also have a start-up program or a primary boot, resulting in the function of "boot by LAN" (Local Area Network), that is, starting the computer via the local network.

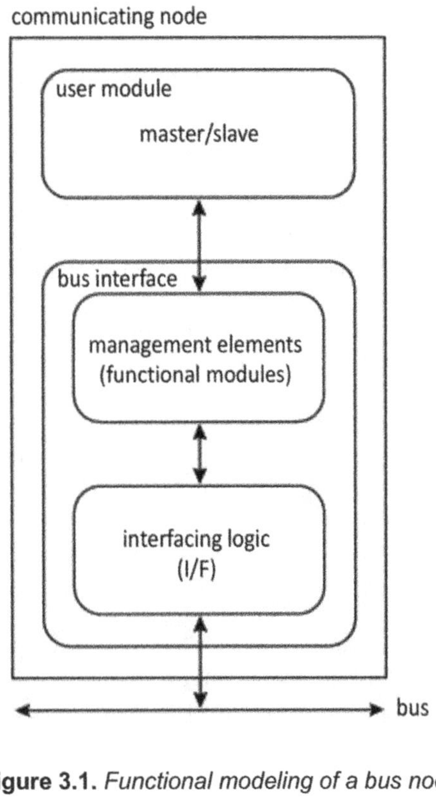

Figure 3.1. *Functional modeling of a bus node*

3.2. Associated signals

A signal is different from the power supply lines (V+, V-, if needed, and Gnd) as it carries information in the shape of a physical parameter: electricity. A signal is said to be unipolar – as opposed to bipolar – when all of its values have the same polarity. Logical signals can be active for a given level (they are "level-sensitive") in the high or low state (positive or negative logic respectively, *cf.* § 2.1.4 in Darche (2004)). They can also be active on one or both edges ("edge-sensitive"). Being active in the low state is marked by the name of a signal (or its acronym), prefixed or suffixed by the symbols n, -, #, * or /, or if it has an upper bar. An absence of symbols, or the + symbol mark activity in the high state. In terms of components, a distinction is made between the Input signal (I), the Output (O) and the input–output.

The signals were initially an amplification of those coming from the microprocessor. In order to make them generic, meaning that they are able to receive electronics that are separate from the electrical interface and the communication protocol of the microprocessor, bus signals are no longer dependent on these elements. An old example was the PCI (Peripheral Component Interconnect, *cf.* § 4.2.4) extension bus, which used to allow the same graphics card to be used by both a Power Mac G4 computer, made by Apple, with a PowerPC G4 microprocessor from Motorola and IBM, and by a PC (Personal Computer) equipped with a microprocessor made by Intel. The only element that changed was the associated device driver (i.e. a system software) because of the different microprocessors and operating systems.

Bus signals are typically separated into different families based on their function. For non-multiplexed buses, a distinction is made between the buses used for transfer, that is, address, data control and transfer state/status/error buses, and the other buses. These "others" are access arbitration, interruption, DMA transfer, synchronization and service buses.

The Address Transfer Bus (ATB) carries the address generated by a master to the slaves in order for them to be chosen. This is the first piece of information sent by the MPU during an access cycle. A position code can assign a unique value to each of the boards that are inserted into the bus (geographical addressing, *cf.* § 1.5).

The Data Transfer Bus (DTB) usually takes on the n signals from the microprocessor D[n-1:0] (also: D_{n-1}-D_0). A data transfer bus can transfer binary words in a smaller format than the format of the bus. This is referred to as a sub-word transfer, for example, 1 byte in a bus with a width of m = 32 bits. In this context, the bus is said to be unjustified – or straight – when the sub-words (the byte in this example) take up the amount of space that they would have taken if they were to belong to a larger word (Figure 3.2(a)). The placements are called lanes or corridors (here "byte lane").

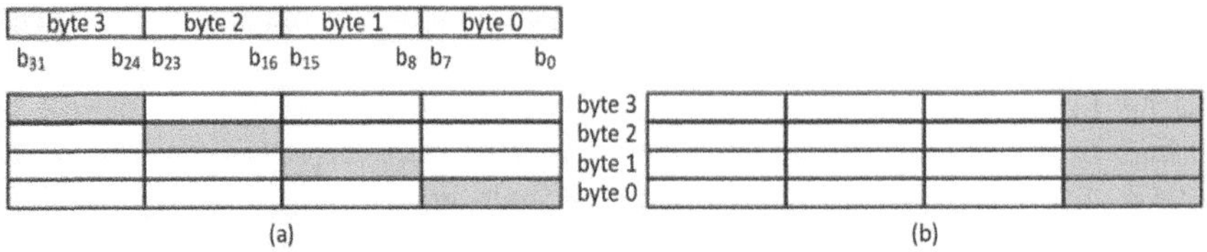

Figure 3.2. *Unjustified bus (a) and justified bus (b) (from Borrill and Theus (1984))*

An example is the synchronous NuBus, created in the 1970s at MIT (Massachusetts Institute of Technology). The concept is illustrated in Figure 3.3.

In a justified bus, the sub-word occupies the extreme bits (which most of the time are those whose weighting is lowest) during transfer; in the end, they are put back in their original position within the module. This is illustrated in Figure 3.2(b). One example is the Multibus-II[1]. A disadvantage is that the associated management electronics, based on multiplexers, is integrated into all of the bus interfaces, even if the nodes respect the native format of the bus. These electronics are complex, expensive and cause delays. In both cases, one or several additional specific signals mark the format of the transfer. Mixed solutions exist for the VME bus (Versa Module European, *cf.* § 4.2.7), with justification for a 16-bit transfer, and a direct version for an 8-bit transfer.

The control bus is made of access control signals (memory and I/O read and write), an additional signal that marks the address type (memory or I/O). It also contains the byte number. The control can mark the valid byte within a word or within the width of the transfer.

The status bus reports on the bus errors. Error signals can involve other masters as well as the memory system. An error can involve address assignment, the information transmitted or stored, the I/O, the power supply management or even the bus itself. The detection and correction of errors is based on the same techniques as those used in the memory, that is, control though Cyclic Redundancy Checks (CRC) (*cf.* § III.6.7 in Darche (2000)), with its own particularity that is logical parity (*cf.* § III.6.6 in Darche (2000) and § 2.6.4 in Darche (2012)). Control can be global, or carried on each word, for example in a subword-parallel transfer.

1 This is a partially justified bus as the 24-bit format transfer is not justified.

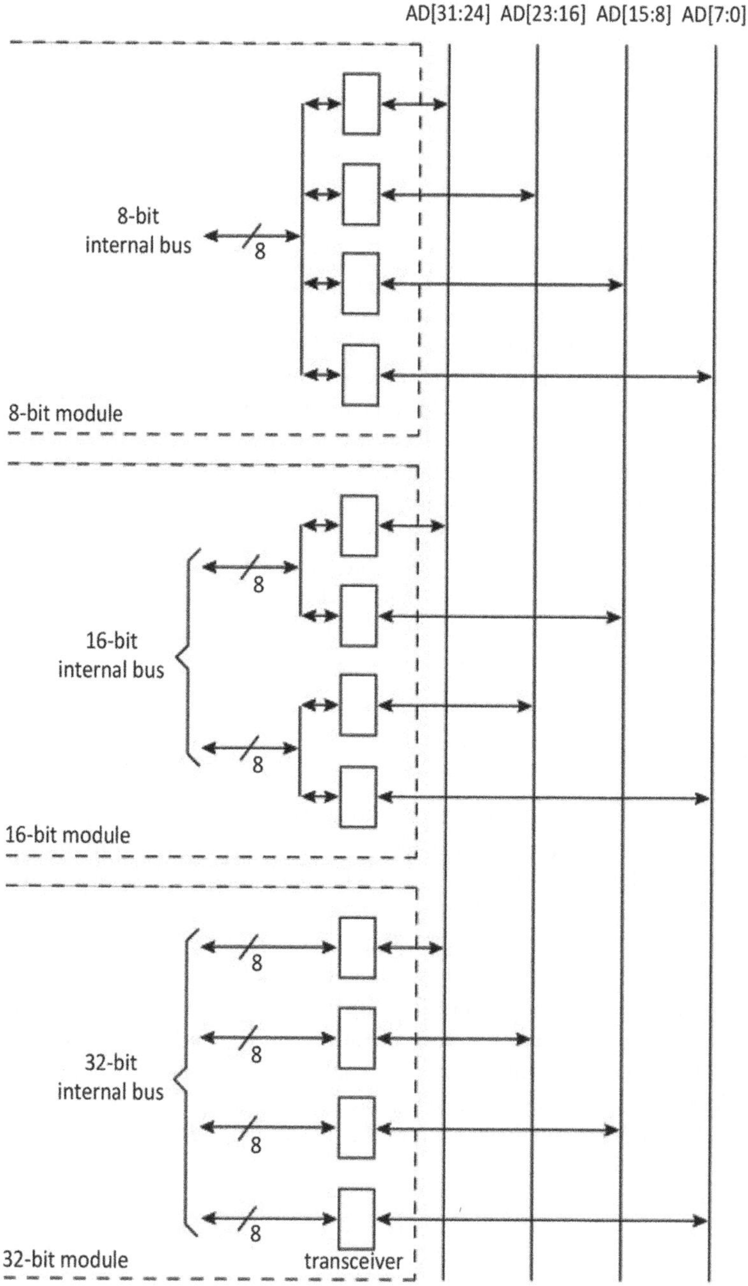

Figure 3.3. *Unjustified bus: Nubus*

The access arbitration bus manages access to the transfer buses. It comprises signals of request, grant and state (locked or relaxed bus). Arbitration can also involve interruption and DMA transfer requests. The signals associated with these belong to the interruption and DMA transfer buses. Interruption management signals are involved in request and acknowledgment. The reset signal (#Reset) is one of these. The DMA transfer bus comprises the direct memory transfer management signals (request and acknowledgment).

The synchronization, or "timing line", bus carries the clock signals (e.g. the "constant clock" and the "bus clock"), the synchronization signals ("strobe" and "transfer acknowledge") and, although only for the pseudo-synchronous bus, the Wait or Ready cycle extension signals. The clock can be asymmetrical, with one edge marking the moment of change, and the other the validity of the information (in order to take it). An example of this type of clock signal is the NuBus.

Lastly, the utility bus generates the start and stop sequences. A specialized slow serial bus can coexist alongside the main bus. It allows management information to be gathered, such as the case in the serial bus of SPB (Serial Presence Detect) memory in SDRAM (Synchronous Dynamic Random Access Memory, *cf.* § 5.3 in Darche (2012)). It allows access to the ROM of modules containing its temporal characteristics, among other things. It can also assume a diagnostic function for bus nodes.

3.3. Interfacing logic

The main purpose of the interfacing logic is to isolate and amplify all of the signals. It can carry out a voltage level shifting between the different types of technology and logical families (i.e. unipolar or bipolar, *cf.* Chapter 2 in Darche (2004)). The logic is made of drivers (line amplifiers) and receivers, which can be coupled together (transceiver, *cf.* § 3.3.4). Due to increases in operating frequency, and in order to provide higher bitrates, "more electronic" functions have been added, such as impedance matching, input filtering – for example, in the case of a wired-OR function – and control of the slew rate at the outputs. When going beyond a few dozen MHz, physical phenomena that could have previously been considered negligible, such as coupling, have to be taken into account. This is of relevance first of all for clock signals and then also for other signal families. This section deals with the specific problems of bus lines.

3.3.1. *Transmission lines*

The path of communication in a bus is embodied materially by an electrical wire, for example, a ribbon cable, or a metallic trace of a Printed Circuit Board (PCB) with return current through the ground, called a transmission line. Four parameters electrically characterize this transmission line. These are: R, a resistance per unit length (unit: Ω/m); L, an inductance per unit length (unit: H/m); C, a capacitance per unit length (unit: C/m); and G, a conductance per unit length (unit: S/m). Figure 3.4 represents this RLCG lumped-parameter model for a short length of cable dx. The value of the resistance is proportional to the length and inversely proportional to the section.

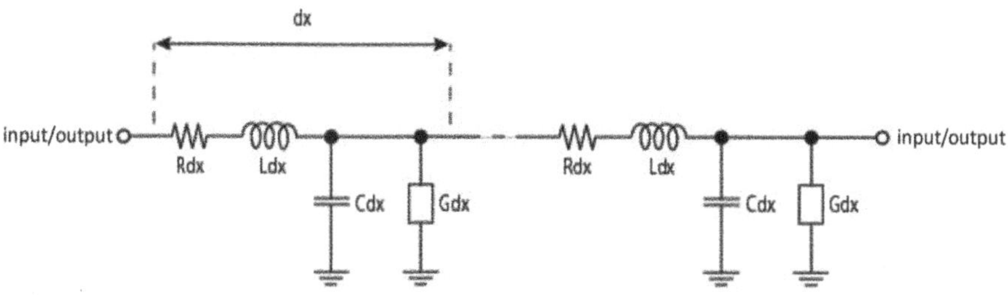

Figure 3.4. *Equivalent circuit of a transmission line (Darche 2004)*

A line has a characteristic impedance Z_0 or Z_c, given in ohms (Ω), which should not be confused with its resistance R, as they both share the same unit. For a line with no losses, it is defined by the following expression:

$$Z_0 = \sqrt{\frac{L_0}{C_0}} \quad [3.1]$$

where L_0 and C_0 are the linear line constants, which are respectively the inductance and the capacitance, per unit of length.

A low frequency line can be considered to be perfect. It is only resistive, as it has no parasitic capacitance or inductance (these values are negligible). At high frequencies, meaning for values of more than one MHz, these secondary characteristics become significant. The propagation velocity v along a line depends on the relative permittivity of the insulation ε_r and it is defined by the following formula, where c is the value of the speed of light:

$$v = \frac{c}{\sqrt{\varepsilon_r}} \quad [3.2]$$

A real computer bus contains several lines with stubs (i.e. derivations). At high frequencies, each connecting pin behaves like an antenna. All kinds of couplings, whether capacitive, inductive or magnetic, can exist. The electric charge for the emitter is not uniform along the bus, and the speed of propagation of the signals is not uniform either. In theory, the propagation time per unit of length t_{po} is given by the following formula:

$$t_{po} = \sqrt{L_0 \times C_0} \qquad [3.3]$$

And the bus delay time t_L with a length of l is equal to:

$$t_L = l \times t_{po} \qquad [3.4]$$

The propagation time t_{po} of a line on an FR4 (Flame Retardant 4) type PCB is in the order of 140–180 ps/inch, which is a little more than twice that of light in a vacuum. The bus can be considered to be a transmission line if the transition time of the signal t_r is less than $2 \times t_L$, as the line effects are no longer negligible, especially those of signal reflection. A quick bus has a fixed value for its length, which is limited. An example of this is the Rambus memory channel (*cf.* § 7.2.1 in Darche (2012)). It should be treated as a collection of transmission lines. The mechanical and electrical characteristics of these lines should be specified. The management electronics should be considered to be more analog than digital. The electronics of the transceivers should be adapted accordingly (*cf.* § 3.3.7).

3.3.2. *Integrity of the signal*

The frequential and temporal features of the communication channel are tied to the electrical parameters of the transmission, which are the value of the resistance, the capacitance and the inductance. Distributed capacitance increases the rise and fall times, which limits bitrate. In order to decrease this time, a driver can be used, but this increases current consumption, as well as noise. The maximum frequency for a coppered pair sits in the order of several dozen GHz. The longer the line and the higher the value of the frequency of the signal, the more there are problems relating to propagation. With every advancing generation of microprocessor, the exchanges of information are carried out at higher and higher frequencies. The first models are used to run at frequencies of less than 1 MHz. Nowadays, these exchanges take place at several hundred megahertz, sometimes even above a GHz for the most powerful models.

This constant race for higher speeds has generated its own electrical problems. Under certain conditions, there can be overshooting and undershooting of the amplitude, as well as ringing signal oscillations. These phenomena take place during changes of the logical state, or when the signal is reflected at the end of line and is overlaid over the incident signal. Issues of crosstalk, that is, interference of one line (the aggressor) on another (the victim), can also arise. Noise interferes with the useful signal and introduces transmission errors. The sources of noise can be RFI (Radio-Frequency Interference) and EMI (ElectroMagnetic Interference, both contained in the field of EMC (ElectroMagnetic Compatibility)), and current loops. One form of protection against electromagnetic interference is shielding. Typically, this is a ground line that is placed between the two signal lines or between the ground planes and the internal power planes. The propagation times acquire the same order of magnitude as the period of the signals, and as a result, management of the clock signals becomes vital. This issue has been examined in § 3.6.5, 3.6.6 and 7.1 in Darche (2012). The interface electronics must take into account the line characteristics in order to specify their own characteristics.

3.3.3. *Terminating a line*

Once it arrives at the end of the line, the signal is reflected. An explanation of this phenomenon can be found in DeFalco (1970). The reflection coefficient Φ can be defined through relation [3.5]. In a short-circuit, Φ = -1, for an open line, Φ = 1 and when impedance is adapted, Φ = 0, so there is no reflection

$$\Phi = \frac{Z_L - Z_0}{Z_L + Z_0} \quad [3.5]$$

where Z_L is the charge at the end of the line.

In order to avoid reflection, the transmission line should end with a termination load R_T. This is either an active or a passive load, whose role is to absorb the energy of the incident signal. In the case of a resistive line, its value must be that of the characteristic impedance of the line Z_0. The first one, which has its resistance in the ground mass (Figure 3.5(a)), is the simplest. The second one (Figure 3.5(b)), whose resistance is connected to a reference potential (the value of which is the median value compared to the electrical current), helps limit any voltage excursions of the signals during commutation, and therefore improves commutation times.

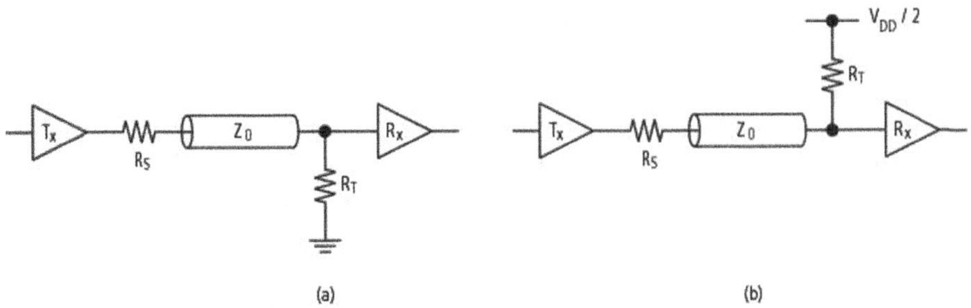

Figure 3.5. *Passive methods of line termination*

The passive approach described above consumes a considerable amount of current. The method in Figure 3.6, based on a voltage divider bridge, is most likely the one that uses the least amount of current.

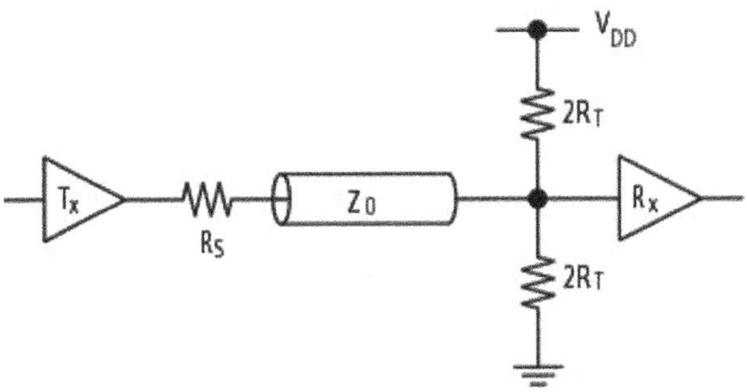

Figure 3.6. *Passive method for terminating a line with a resistive voltage divider bridge (continued)*

Figure 3.7(a) and (b) shows an applied example of SSTL (Stub Series Terminated Logic, *cf.* § 3.4 in Darche (2012)).

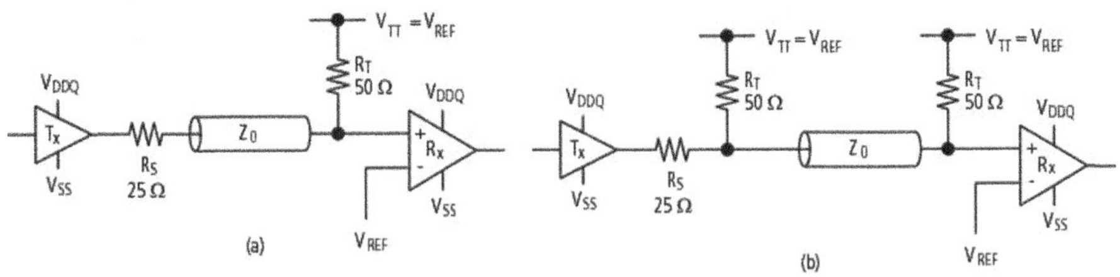

Figure 3.7. *Diagrams of passive terminations in SSTL_2 classes I (a) and II (b)*

A reference tension V_{ref} of 0.7 V helps limit the sub-voltages to roughly 0 V (pinch-off voltage). This is what happens in the Eurobus bus, which relies on the direct voltage V_d of the clamping diode when it is conducting (Figure 3.8).

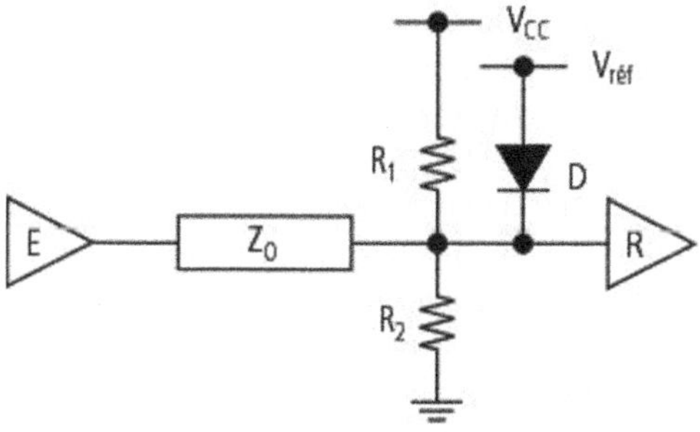

Figure 3.8. *Undervoltage diode limiter (active approach)*

Active approaches, which use voltage or current regulators, are preferred. These are shown in Figure 3.9.

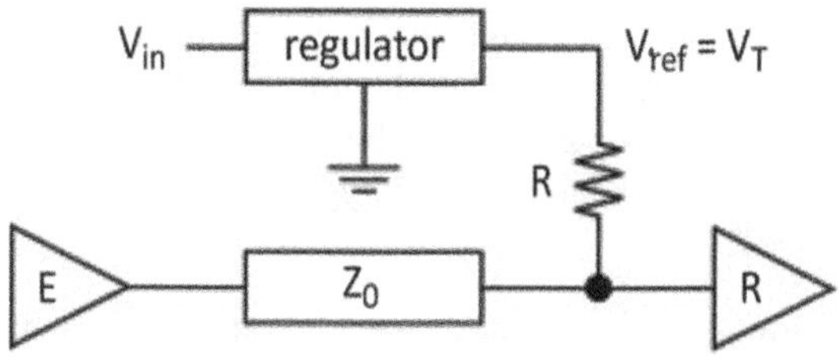

Figure 3.9. *Active line termination based on a voltage regulator*

In order to remove static consumption, an AC termination (Alternating Current) based on an RC (Resistor–Capacitor) serial network can be considered.

3.3.4. *Driver and receiver*

In order to transmit a signal along the bus, an emitter tasked with amplifying the signal (a line or bus driver) and a receiver are required. The emitter sees the line and the receiver as electrical loads. When there is only one wire, this is called a single-wire system. In order to emit and receive when in full-duplex, two lines are needed. This is called a two-wire system. The receiver interprets the signal voltage by comparing it to one or several reference voltages in order to determine what the corresponding logical state is.

With regard to the electrics, short-circuits can occur along the lines of a bus when two entities deliver complementary states at their outputs. This issue can be fixed through the notion of logical gate output with an open collector, emitter, drain or source, depending on the technology used, as well as with the inaccurately named "three-state" logic (or TRI-STATE® logic, *cf.* § 2.2.1 in Darche (2004)). The first type of output is usually well-adapted for arbitration and buses, as it is less sensitive to design errors. Unlike in a three-state output, a short-circuit resulting from two outputs being active in complementary states (one in the state "1" and the other in the state "0") is not possible here. It enables a bus connection to be created. These outputs also establish a wired-AND in active-high logic and a wired-OR in active-low logic (*cf.* § 3.4.5 in Darche (2004)). However, they require the presence of a voltage-pulling system that can either be passive (resistance) or active (Pull-Up or Pull-Down Network (PUN or PDN) *cf.* § 2.1.1 in Darche (2004)). One major disadvantage is the presence of glitches, which can even result in the generation of unwanted logical states (wire(d)-OR glitch) when the output transistor of the driver switches to its ON-state in a large enough bus (Gustavson and Theus 1983). A filter must be put in place in order to eliminate, or at least attenuate, these glitches. The output of a three-state logical operator allows for a bus element to be electrically disconnected. Its output stage is of the "push–pull" type, with an adequate command that allows the two output transistors to be blocked. There are therefore three possible states, two low-impedance states high (H) and low (L), and one high-impedance state (Z or Hi-Z).

This specialized management logic of access and exchanges between the entity (MPU, memory or I/O exchange unit) and the bus is integrated into the bus interface. Connection and disconnection of the entity to the bus is carried out using a buffer (Figure 3.10), which also belongs to this subset that allows the bus to be shared. When flow is permitted in both directions, it is called a transceiver (a contraction of the terms transmitter and receiver). The command signals of the bus interfaces are generated from the control and status signals coming from the master (i.e. the microprocessor), or even from the bus controller. In the case of a three-state logic, the connection of the outputs of the transmitting buffers to the bus is controlled by their #OE (Output Enable) signal, which allows movement from the high impedance state to the low impedance state. Note that the direction in which the information travels is exclusively determined by this same signal when it is active, either for the output buffer, or for the input buffer of the bus interface.

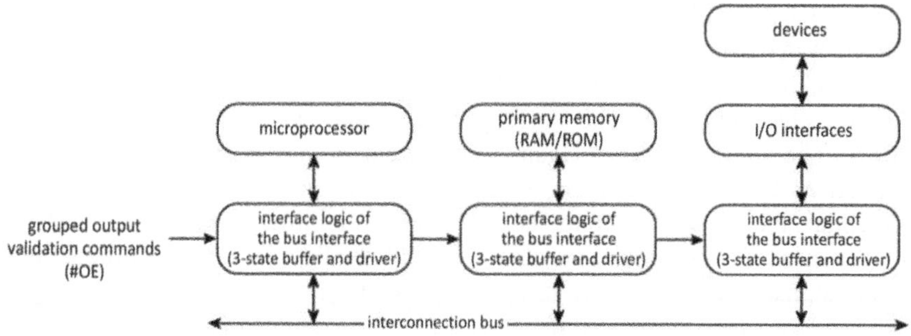

Figure 3.10. *Connecting to the buses with a buffer*

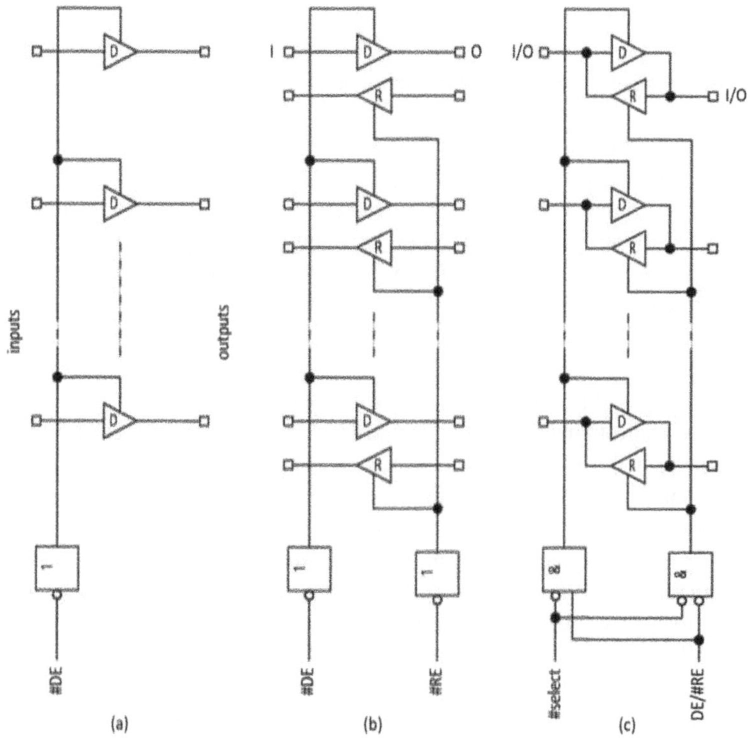

Figure 3.11. *Difference between a buffer and a transceiver*

Strictly speaking, what distinguishes the transceiver (Figure 3.11(c)) from the bidirectional buffer (Figure 3.11(b)) are the driver D/receiver R couples, which are connected head to tail, and an antagonist command of their three-state outputs. This has been covered in Darche (2004). The bidirectional buffer separately groups the commands of the driver outputs (#DE (Driver Enable)) and the receiver outputs (#RE (Receiver Enable)). The buffer also exists as a one-way version (Figure 3.11(a)). The logical operators can be inverters or not inverters. The driver is characterized by special functions, such as a shift in the voltage level (i.e. a change of potential, the relevant operator is called a "level shifter", *cf.* § 3.8.2 in Darche (2004)), whose fanout is high in order to "attack" the line. To limit the production of parasitic signals along the adjacent lines (crosstalk) due to state changes along the capacitive line, one solution that does not affect the data rate is to limit the slew rate of the output voltage of the line drivers, and to add a low-pass filter at the input of the receivers, which acts as a noise rejecter, limiting noise. The components involved in implementing this solution are called "trapezoidal" drivers, because of the limited slope of the signals.

3.3.5. *Differential and single-ended links*

Electrically speaking, a link between two points can be 'Single-Ended' (SE) (also called an "unbalanced transmission"). This means that it has only one conductor, which carries a signal whose voltage is referenced to a shared reference rail, which usually tends to be the ground. One advantage of single-ended links is their simplicity, which reduces costs. Only one wire is needed per signal, on top of which a shared reference rail must be added, which is the ground (Figure 3.12). The use of the ground as a reference means that there can be jumps in voltage (ground bounced), caused by current consumption peaks. This reference must have as low an impedance as possible; otherwise, current returns run the risk of generating a differential voltage that is too high, thus reducing the noise margin (*cf.* § 2.2.1 in Darche (2004)). All of this means that the link is not very resilient to noise. For high frequencies, the capacitive and inductive electrical couplings, and the magnetic coupling between links that was previously negligible, start to be significant. Transients appear, introducing crosstalk. The characteristic impedance of the line Z_0 must also be taken into account, as a mismatch would lead to signal reflection at the end of the line. Moreover, the additional presence of the sharp rising (also called positive) and falling (also called negative) edges of the rapid digital signals results in the creation of over- and undervoltages. These phenomena are critical for short lines. In a noisy environment where the frequency is high, a twisted-pair cable must be used, the cable must be shielded electromagnetically and additional ground lines must be used, which will act as an electromagnetic shield, and the impedance must be lowered. All of this obviously contributes to the overall cost.

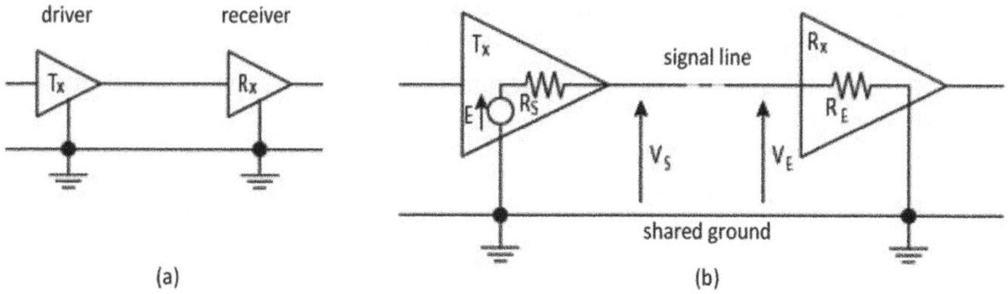

Figure 3.12. *Single-ended link (unbalanced) and its electrical model*

In order to improve these issues, the differential link (also called "balanced" link, or "symmetrical transmission") uses two wires (Figure 3.13). Both solutions can be grouped together with an asymmetrical driver and a differential receiver, under the standard TIA/EIA 423 (TIA 2001). The receiver can have a fully differential input, or, less commonly, a pseudo-differential input[2], as can be found in Analog-to-Digital Converters (ADC) (*cf.* § 3.5.1 in Darche (2003). When the number of signals to be carried is equal to n, then n + 1 wires are required for the single-ended link if using a shared ground (which is most of the time). However, for a high bitrate, a signal return is still necessary. In a differential link, the number of wires needed is equal to $(2 \times n) + 1$.

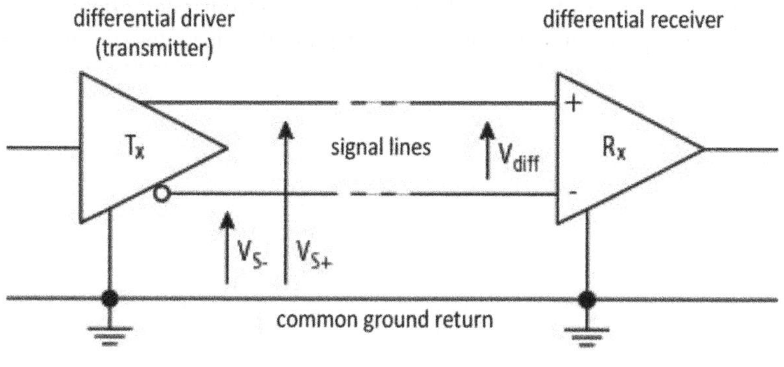

Figure 3.13. *Differential link (no link)*

One version of the differential transceiver (Figure 3.14(a)) transforms the differential signal of the link or of the bus into a unipolar signal. In version (b), the

2 Fully differential and pseudo-differential inputs differ in the presence of grounds that are differentiated from the signal and from the converter.

input of the driver is no longer linked to the output of the receptor, and their output commands are no longer shared (a less strict definition of a transceiver, *cf.* § 3.3.4), which opens up the possibility for the designer to return to version (a) through the corresponding wirings.

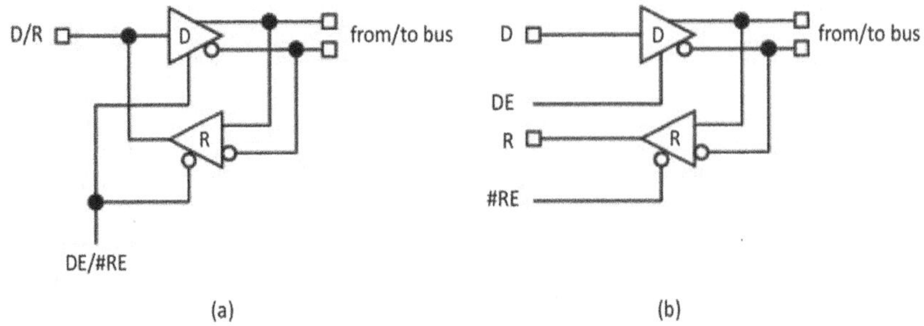

Figure 3.14. *Differential transceivers*

The layout of the differential link (lower part of Figure 3.15) makes it less sensitive to common-mode noise than an asymmetrical link (higher part of the same figure). Any electromagnetic interference (EMI) appears as having the same polarity (common-mode voltage) along both lines (Figure 3.15(b), lower illustration) and is cancelled by the receiver, which subtracts one signal from the other. Moreover, it radiates less as a result of the cancelling out of the electromagnetic fields. However, it has the same requirements with regard to adapting the characteristic impedance in order to avoid any signal reflection.

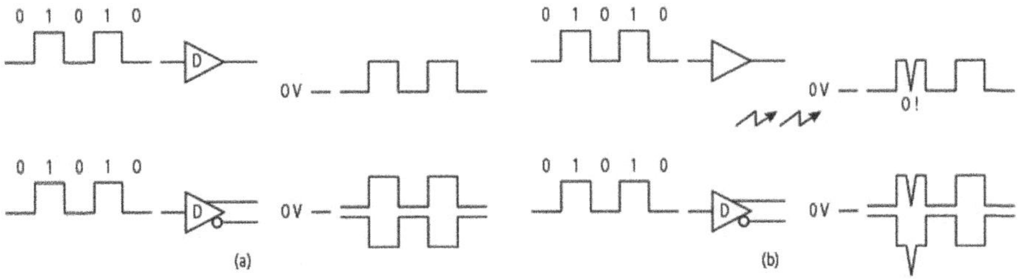

Figure 3.15. *Noise in the asymmetrical transmission lines (upper half) and differential transmission lines (lower half)*

3.3.6. *Topologies*

Let us consider for the moment that a communication point is either a driver or a receiver. When there are only two points communicating, therefore necessarily one driver and one receiver, this is called a point-to-point link[3] (or "simplex"). When there are more than two, this is called multipoint-to-multipoint topology (or "multiplex"). The classic topologies are the bus (Figure 3.16 for the asymmetrical version) and the daisy chain. In the case of the bus, the communication medium is shared.

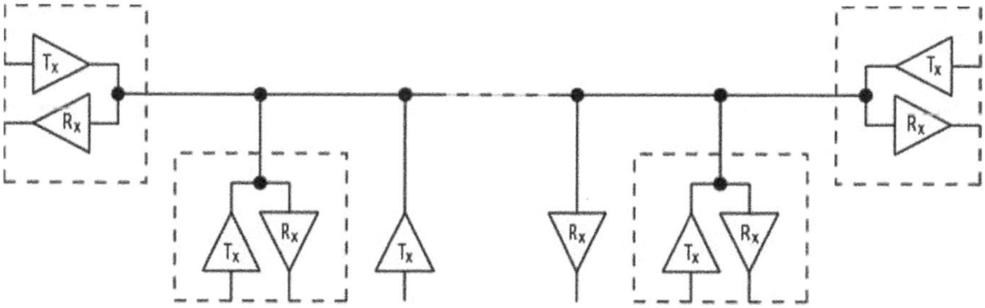

Figure 3.16. *Bidirectional link or asymmetrical type multipoint bus*

Figure 3.17 presents the differential version of the multipoint bus.

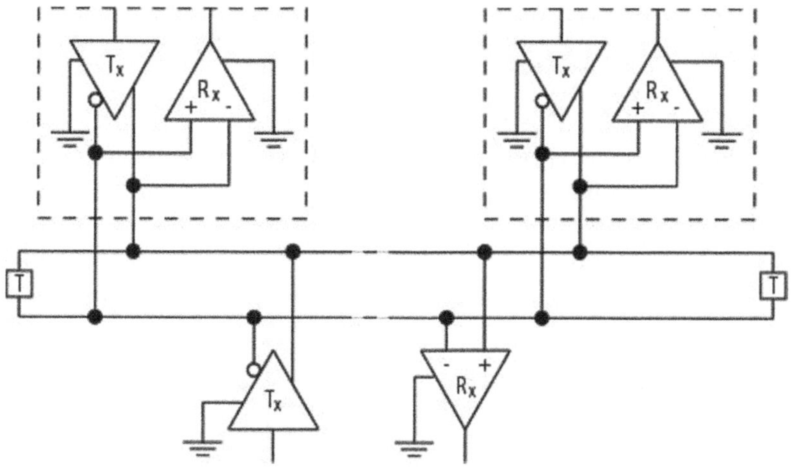

Figure 3.17. *Bidirectional link, or differential type multipoint bus*

One variant is the "multidrop" topology ("point-to-multipoint" or "distributed simplex"), where a single driver sends the signal to several receivers (at least two).

3 This can also be called "single-drop bus", that is, a bus with a master and only one slave.

The driver can be placed at the end of the line (Figure 3.18(a)), or in the middle (Figure 3.18(b)), in order to minimize the propagation time t_L and, consequently, the flight time t_{flight} (*cf.* § 1.2) of the signal.

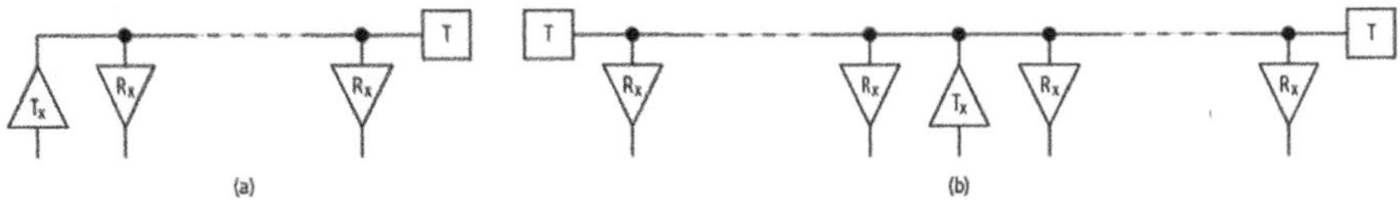

Figure 3.18. *One-directional links (multidrop) with single end (a) and double end (b)*

Figure 3.19 shows the differential version of a bus with a "multidrop" topology.

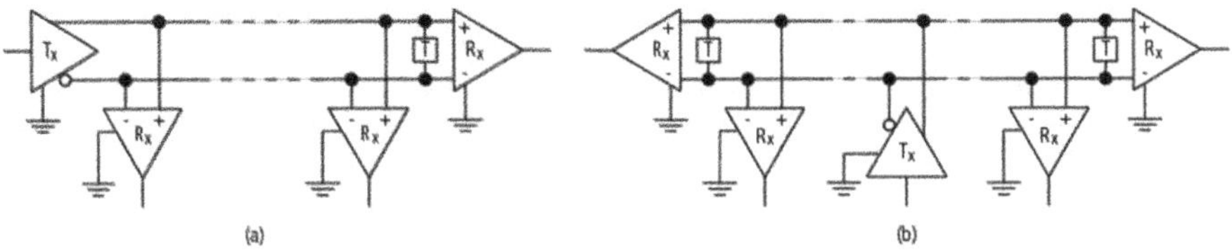

Figure 3.19. *One-directional links (multidrop) with single end (a) and double end (b)*

The advantage of this approach is diffusion. The connections seen in Figure 3.20 help establish a multidrop connection.

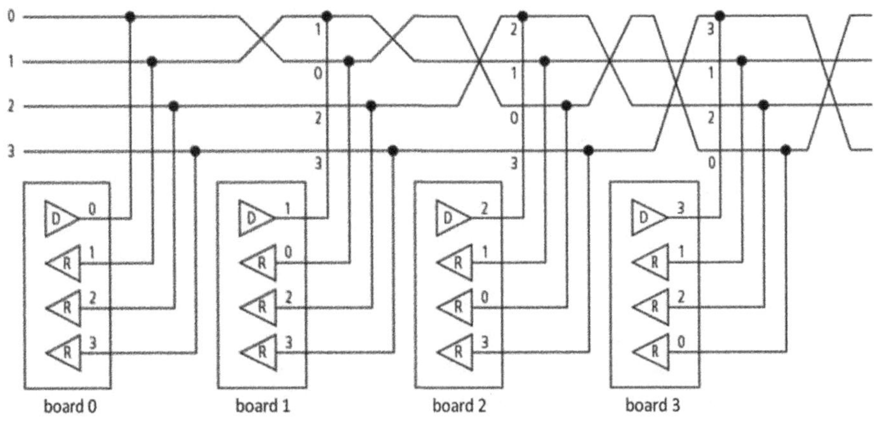

Figure 3.20. *Connection in a multidrop bus (from Strassberg (1999))*

A final version is the switched point-to-point bus. The gate, or communication matrix, in Figure 3.21 can only connect an input I_j to a single output O_k with i, k ∈ [0, 3] and j ≠ k (so no backlooping possible). The advantage is that the communication is full-duplex, and, electrically speaking, there are no stubs, as they are point-to-point links. The disadvantage is the presence of a switch in the middle of the bus, which is a sensitive node for communication.

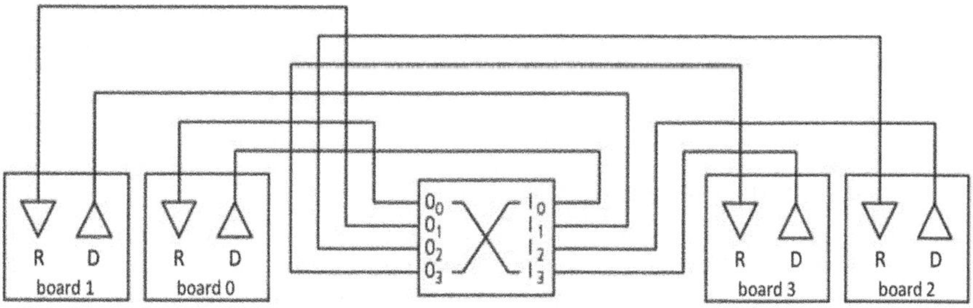

Figure 3.21. *Switching matrix enabling communication between the electronic boards of a bus*

Instead of sharing a channel, point-to-point connections can be considered using an approach based on circuit-switching networks and packet-switching networks. In the latter, there is no established circuit, so no time is lost establishing it. Of the two, it is the more tolerant to faults, and reordering of the packets is possible.

3.3.7. *Electronic technologies*

From a logic technology point of view (*cf.* (Darche 2004)), transceivers belong first and foremost to the group of discrete connected logical components. An example of bipolar technology is the ECL (Emitter Coupled Logic), which is a rapid open-emitter logic. Otherwise, these are logics that derive from TTL (Transistor–Transistor Logic), such as the FAST (Fairchild Advanced Schottky TTL). MOS-bipolar mixed technologies such as the BCT (BiCMOS Technology) have helped lower electrical consumption and increase switch speed. Nowadays, they are becoming specialized. Examples are the CMOS GTL (Gunning Transceiver Logic) family (Gunning 1991; JEDEC 2007) and the GTLP (GTL Plus[4]) family made by the company Fairchild, and presented in § 1.5.4 and 2.5.4 in Darche (2004). Technologies that were specially developed for backplane buses include the BTL (Backplane Transceiver Logic) by the company National Semiconductor (NS),

4 Intel has developed its own improved GTL, called GTL+ (Intel 1997), for its Pentium microprocessor range.

introduced in 1984, as well as its version of CMOS, called CBTL (CMOS BTL). Others were developed for memory interfaces on the channel. Examples include RSL (Rambus Signaling Level) logic for Rambus memories, and SSTL for SDRAM (*cf.* § 3.4 in Darche (2012)). As the supply voltage is decreased in order to reduce power consumption as well as electromagnetic interference, following a differential approach, bus technologies have been derived from LVDS (Low-Voltage Differential (LVD) Signaling, standard TIA/EIA-644) technology through the BLVDS (Bus LVDS) by the company NS, as well as the LVDM (LVD Multipoint) by Texas Instruments (TI). M-LVDS (Multipoint-LVDS) is the normalized version of this (ANSI/TIA/EIA 2002).

3.4. Insertion-withdrawal under tension

Some advanced functions have made their appearance, such as live insertion-withdrawals, or hot plugs/hot swap capabilities. These allow for the insertion of electronic subunits without having to power down first. This is particularly useful in a server that has to have high rates of availability. The function itself can be applied to an I/O interface (*cf.* § 2.2 in Darche (2003). The USB (Universal Serial Bus) is an example of this. In this way, a device can be (dis)connected without cutting off the power supply and without disturbing the Operating System (OS). The insertion of an electronic board into a powered system can result in electrical interference at the level of the signals (glitches) and of the supply, which can even lead to the destruction of electrical components, particularly the I/O stages of the interface logic of the transceivers, as an example (*cf.* § 3.5.1 in Darche (2003)). One of the causative phenomena is called "latch-up" (*cf.* § 3.5.1 in Darche (2004)), which is the parasitic powering-on of thyristors formed of parasitic transistors. This can be avoided by having a power-on sequence (*cf.* § V3-6.1.3 on power supply profiles). Live withdrawal or insertion characterizes the ability to insert or disconnect a component or electronic subset – here a bus – without having to first turn off the power supply of the system and without disturbing its operation. The integrity of the data is also preserved. This hardware functionality makes maintenance easier and quicker. Subsequently, recognition and initialization of the board has to be handled at a software level, for example, through the operating system. The OS must also detect any disconnection of a node in order to take suitable measures, such as ejecting a device.

There are several levels of electrical protections. Soltero and Cox (2002) list four levels of isolation. Level 0 shows that there is no way of inserting an electronic board with the power on without risking destruction of the component parts. In level 1 ("partial power down"), a board can be inserted with the power on, but the receiver must first put all of its output signals under high impedance. The board contains eddy-current limiters. Level 2 ("hot plugging", "insertion" or "swapping") goes further than the previous level, with a high impedance guarantee, varying from 0 V up to a threshold voltage. The validity of the exchanges is not always ensured, however. The final level ("live insertion") overcomes this limitation. The data is not corrupted.

3.5. Test and debugging

Debugging a bus can be done by analyzing transaction traces, either in real-time or post-hoc, using generalized measuring devices such as an oscilloscope, or with specialized devices like the logic analyzer, which integrates the protocol.

Moreover, there are dedicated buses available for the hardware and software debugging of computer systems or single components, such as a processor or a SoC (System on (a) Chip). Examples include the JTAG bus (Joint Test Action Group, IEEE reference 1149.1 (IEEE 2013)). This aspect is covered in detail in § V5-2.2.5.

3.6. Bus limits

The limit of a classical bus (i.e. a data/address/control bus with cycle-based communication) is the dispersion of electrical and temporal characteristics. Figure 3.22 shows this grid distribution of the signal of a classic memory subset that uses memory sticks. There are three distinct signal types: address, control and data (DQ).

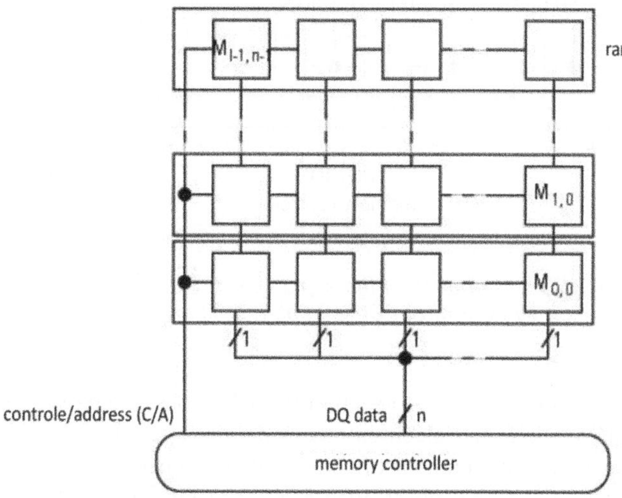

Figure 3.22. *Distribution of signals in a memory subset with communication by cycle (from Crisp et al. (1997) and Ware et al. (2001))*

Looking more closely at the SDRAM version (Figure 3.23), these three buses are the DQ/DQM data bus, the control bus represented by the #RAS (Row Address Strobe), #CAS (Column Address Strobe) and #CE (Chip Enable), and the address bus A. The clock signal, like the address, must reach each component. By measuring each bus and each line of these buses, it becomes apparent that the signal path lengths are not identical for all of the signals, and that the number of connected pins is not the same. This will have consequences for the electrical and temporal characteristics of these buses, which will end up being different.

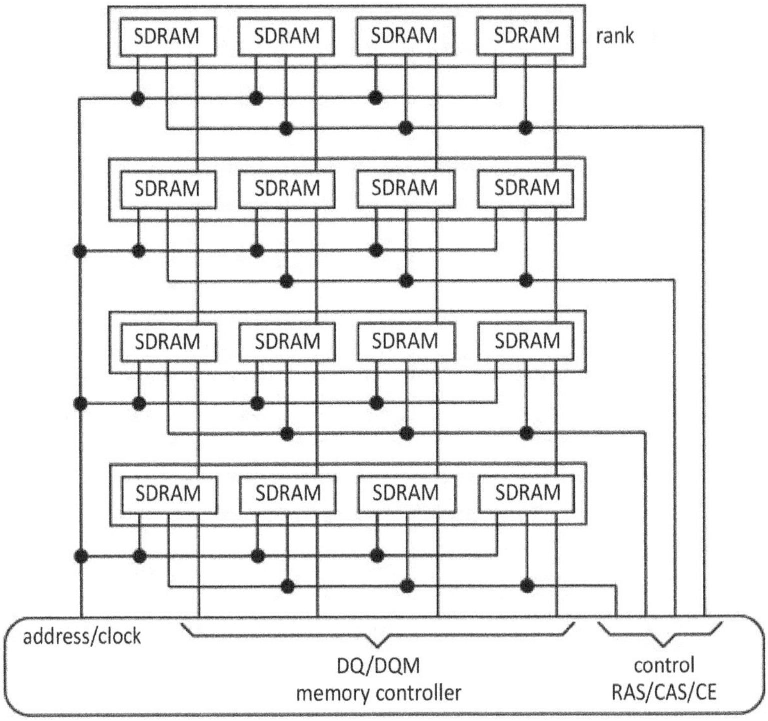

Figure 3.23. *Distribution of the signals in an SDRAM subset with communication by cycle (from Crisp et al. (1997) and Ware et al. (2001))*

Figure 3.24 shows how, for an (a)synchronous memory device with communication by cycle, the electrical and temporal characteristics of a bus line change as a function of the number of connected components, that is, as a function of the storage capacity of the subset. Electrically speaking, these characteristics are the resistance, the inductance and the capacitance. The characteristic impedance, and thus the reflection coefficient, can vary. This results in an impedance mismatch. For the time being, this affects mostly the rise and fall times and the propagation time. Progression is linear for all signals apart from the control signal as they are distributed between all of the components. The control is unique for each row. Moreover, the memories can have different storage capacities. Also, the output drivers usually have different fan-outs (*cf.* § 2.2.1 in Darche (2004)) and input/output impedances. A solution to this issue of disparity of the bus characteristics is provided by the company Rambus and involves encapsulating all of these signals into an information packet that is to be carried by a bus whose electrical and temporal characteristics are uniform.

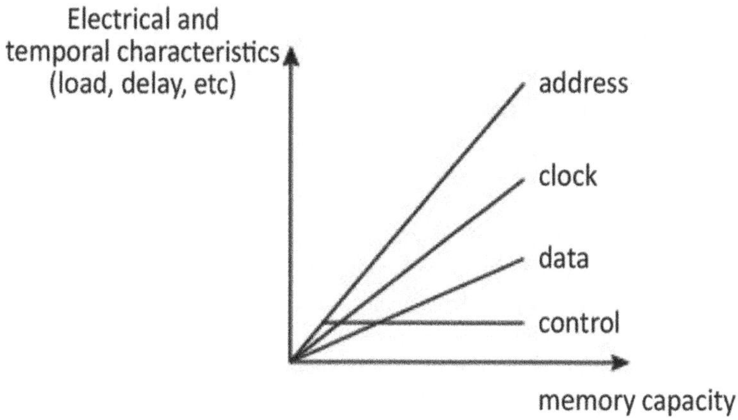

Figure 3.24. *Evolution of the electrical and temporal characteristics of a bus line as a function of the number of components (adapted from Crisp (1997))*

An example of an optimized storage bus is the Rambus channel. The name of this interface is that of the company that created it. As a result, it is owned, patented and non-standardized, which has led to commercial disputes and resulted in lawsuits with other memory device producers (Stern 2001a, 2001b, 2001c, 2002, 2003, 2007, 2009). It was described for the first time by Kushiyama *et al.* (1992) and Slater (1992). The physical communication medium is made of a data bus, two command signals, BusCtrl and BusEnable, as well as two clock signals, ClkFromMaster and ClkToMaster. All of these signals taken together form a Rambus channel. This channel has more than 32 slave nodes, which are managed by a channel master (Figure 3.25), and is terminated by a "terminating load". A channel slave can only be a memory device. The channel master is the only entity that can send requests. The master is usually a memory controller, but it can also be a processor or an I/O controller.

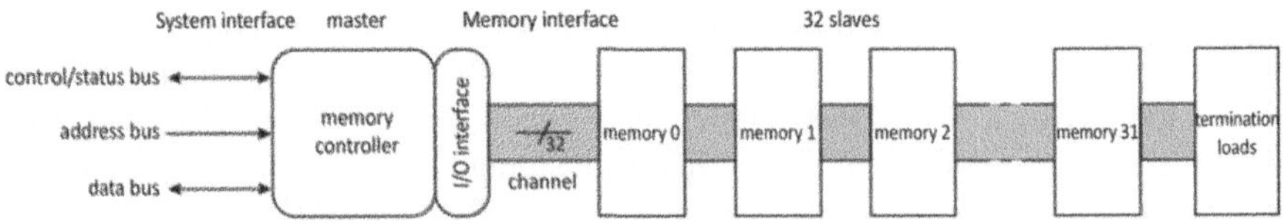

Figure 3.25. *The original version of the Rambus channel*

The channel lines, which are separated by a ground line in order to form an electromagnetic shield to avoid coupling, are routed in parallel on the printed circuit. Each trace that carries a signal can electrically be considered as a transmission line. As a result, each bus line has the same electrical characteristics (characteristic impedance, capacitance, inductance, etc.) and temporal characteristics (propagation time, etc.). Moreover, the line drivers have the same fanout and the same output impedance, and they can see the same length of line. This means the characteristics change in the same way at the same time (Figure 3.26), which was not the case when using the approaches above, where they changed by group or by category (i.e. the bus type) as memory devices were inserted onto the bus (Figure 3.24). In order to avoid any reflection of the incident signal at the end of the line, an active resistive load (made of transistors, for example) or a passive one (resistor, inductor or capacitor) is placed at each extremity of the channel.

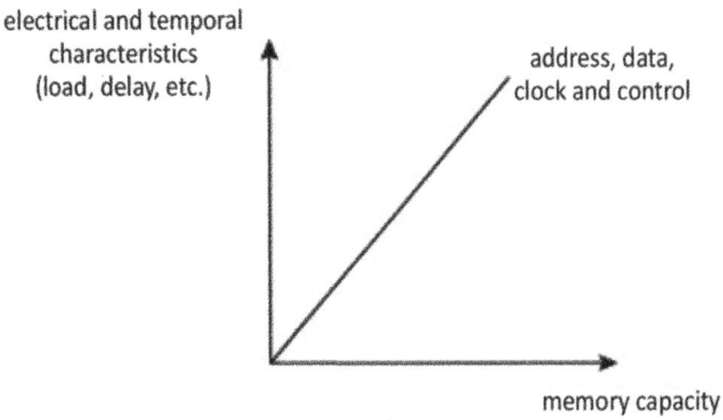

Figure 3.26. *Evolution of the electrical and temporal characteristics of a channel line as a function of the number of chips in the channel (adapted from Crisp (1997))*

The current trend is for serial point-to-point connections. By increasing the number of links or channels, the format n of the information also goes up. Link buses are an example of this (*cf.* § 4.2.3).

3.7. Conclusion

This chapter has covered the aspects of interfacing of a one-bus logical module. After examining the signals of different buses, we looked at electronic notions such as the transmission line, signal integrity, line termination and drivers. To finish off, specific themes such as powered insertion/withdrawal, or the test, were covered.

4

Bus Classifications

The primary purpose of this chapter is to present the different topologies of bus-based architectures. It also covers buses currently used in the computer industry.

4.1. Multibus architecture

Initially, all the entities shared the same bus, called a "shared bus", or "linear bus" (DEC PDP-11 vocabulary), when there was only one bus connecting all of the subunits inside a computer (CPU for Central Processing Unit), memory, devices and the display terminal). All sorts of information and signals would pass through this bus, at variable bitrates. Table 4.1 gives a summary of the exchanges between masters and slaves.

Transfer from/to	CPU	Memory	I/O
CPU	Interrupt request message	Medium bitrate information (data)	I/O control/command Low bitrate information
Memory	Medium bitrate information (instruction and data)	High bitrate information (DMA transfer/burst)	High bitrate information (DMA transfer/burst)
Input/Output (I/O)	Status of the I/O Low bitrate information interrupt request	High bitrate information (DMA transfer/burst)	High bitrate information (DMA transfer/burst)

Table 4.1. *Exchange types between the master and the slave*

Despite mechanisms such as the interrupt request or Direct Memory Access (DMA, *cf.* § 2.2.2), and with the ever-rising speeds of the central units, isolation of the slower entities – that is, the I/O and the memories – has become a necessity. The natural consequence of this process has been the splitting of buses into several levels, depending on the number of nodes. This is known as a multi-tiered bus architecture, and relates to the processor bus, with its low latency and a high bitrate, the memory bus with a high bitrate, and the I/O controller bus. A bus that is local to the microprocessor allows it to communicate with a single coprocessor or cache controller. The size of each of the buses is tied to the bitrates or to the type of entities connected. Separation of the buses helps decrease the latency and increases the bandwidth. This approach is called functional partitioning. There is also an electronic justification for this partitioning. The number of logical inputs and outputs that are connected is limited by the fan-in and fan-out of logic gates (*cf.* § 2.2.1 in Darche (2004)). Figure 4.1 demonstrates this concept through a presentation of the organization of buses in a microcomputer such as the PC XT ("Personal Computer eXtended Technology", *cf.* § V5-3.2.1), made by the company IBM. The term "local bus" refers to the bus at the level of the microprocessor, hence the alternative name of "processor bus". A bridge connects the processor bus to the "extension bus", which allows the entities of the two buses to communicate.

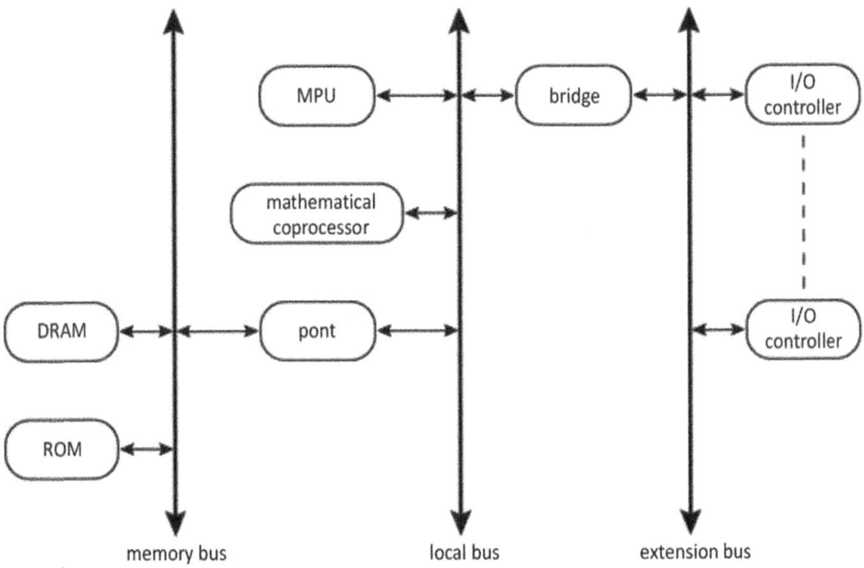

Figure 4.1. *Layout of communication in a PC XT microcomputer*

A commercial example of this is the Multibus II, made by Intel, which has five buses (Figure 4.2). The iPSB™ (Parallel System Bus) and the iSSB™ (Serial System Bus) establish communication between the cards of a system. Together, they form the communications "backbone" of the system. The multichannel iLBX™, iSBX™ and DMA buses help expand the available functions of a card. The iLBX™ II bus (Local Bus Extension), or the memory-only execution bus, is reserved for memory expansions. The iSBX™ (Single Board Bus) allows a mezzanine card to be connected to the expansion card. The Multichannel™ I/O bus allows direct transfers to be made between the memory and the I/O.

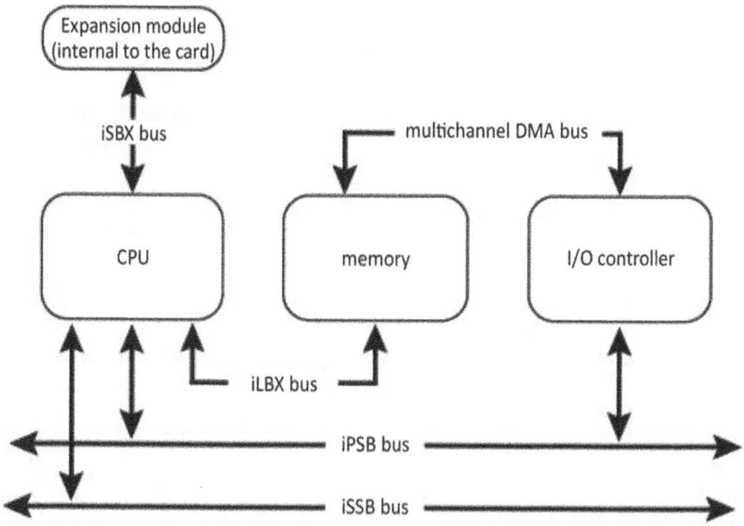

Figure 4.2. *Architecture of the Multibus II*

4.1.1. *Segmented buses*

Many researchers and engineers have come up with a number of different types of interconnections in order to determine their properties. Figure 4.3 illustrates the example of a split – or "segmented" – bus. Each segment is a portion of a bus. This is the logical unit of bus splitting, allowing communication between the masters M and the slaves S. It comprises the classical line terminations. The segments communicate via the signal repeaters R. Given that both the length of each segment and the number of nodes are reduced, the loads – whether parasitic in nature, or not – are also reduced, resulting in a reduction in switching noise and in power consumption. Propagation times also go down. This approach is best used in asynchronous buses.

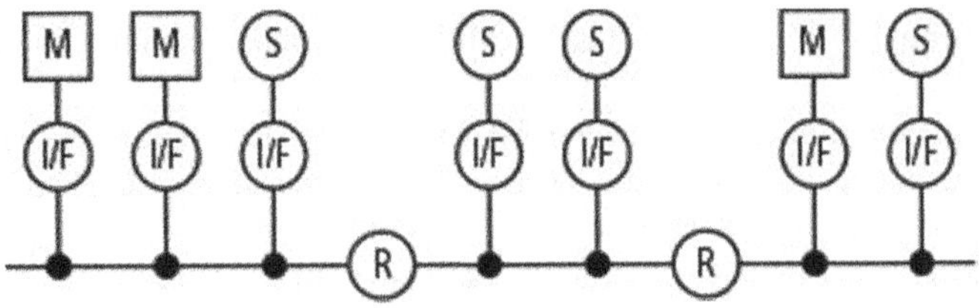

Figure 4.3. *Serially segmented buses*

4.1.2. *Hierarchical buses*

A variation here is the hierarchy of segmented buses (Figure 4.4). A cluster of elements communicates through a locally segmented bus. The local buses are linked together by the global bus. The bus shown in bold is the inter-cluster bus. All of these buses taken together form what is known as a *bus hierarchy*. This is a partial solution to the issue of overly long buses, which have negative effects, both temporally and electrically. This approach also increases the total bitrate, capability and reliability.

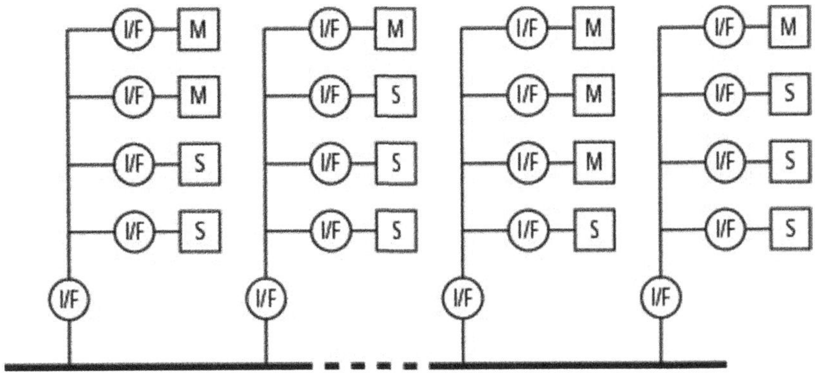

Figure 4.4. *Segmented bus hierarchy (Borrill 1988)*

This structure can be generalized to more than two levels, forming a generalized bus hierarchy, illustrated in Figure 4.5. This is also referred to as a clustered bus arrangement. The locality of the communication and the bitrate are the typical criteria for defining this hierarchy. Other criteria such as the type of elements linked together can also be taken into account (*cf.* § 4.2). Care must be taken with regard to bus multiplexing on several levels – if buses are not multiplexed, this can result in time-consuming (de)multiplexing operations.

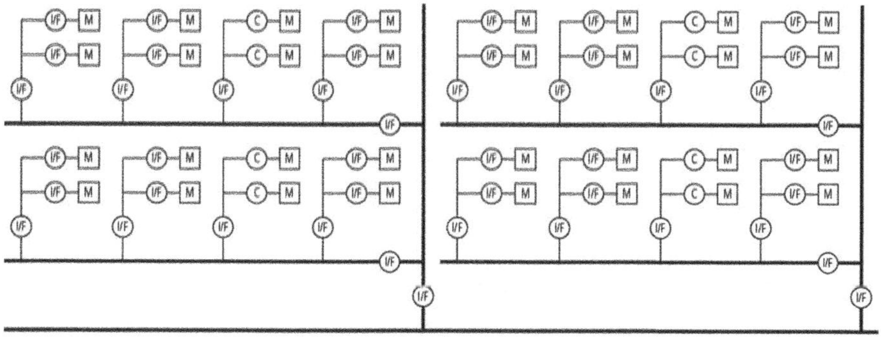

Figure 4.5. *Generalized bus hierarchy*

Figure 4.6 presents a topology for shared memories, adapted to a parallel architecture.

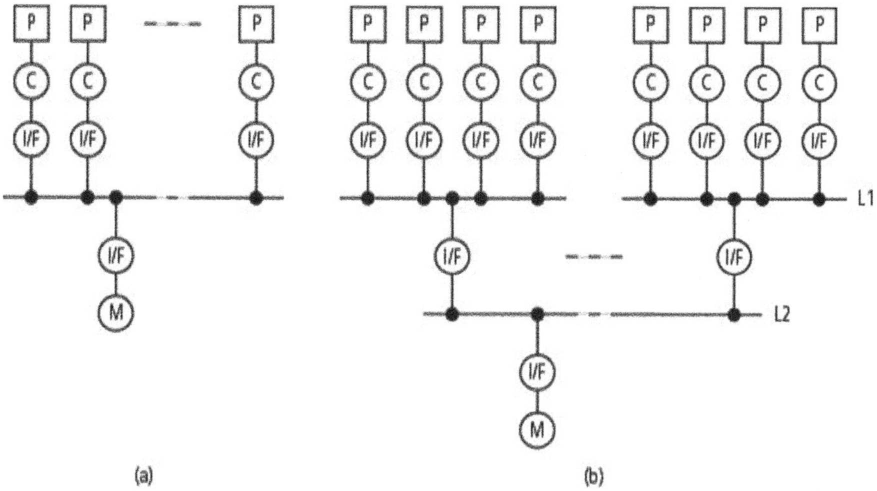

Figure 4.6. *Classical (a) and hierarchical (b) shared memory and bus topologies*

4.1.3. *Multiple buses*

In the 1980s, research focused on parallel architecture for calculators using multiple processors, multiple storage systems and multiple buses. The term "parallel buses" has been used before, but in order to avoid confusion, we have favored the term "multiple buses", in reference to the number of communication channels (*cf.* § 1.2), as shown in Figure 4.7. Multiple buses allow for concurrent communication to take place. The notion of hierarchy can also be applied here.

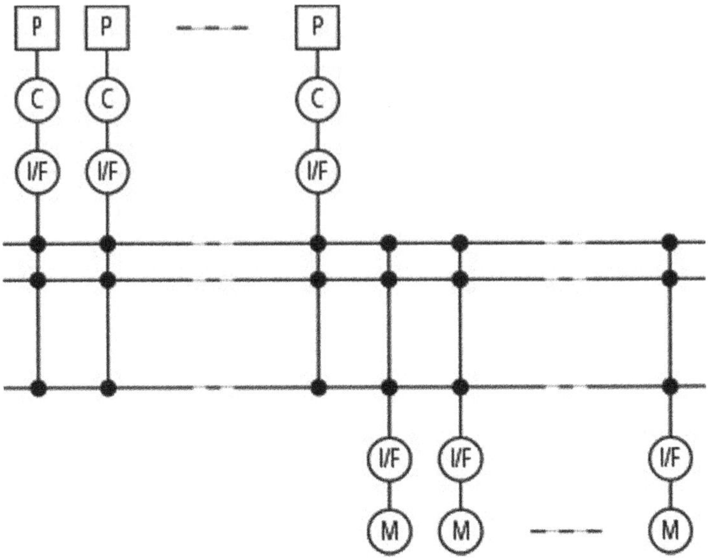

Figure 4.7. *Topology with multiple buses for a multiprocessor architecture*

There are other forms of interconnection topologies, such as the grid, or multistage interconnection networks. These are especially used in SoCs (System on (a) Chip), *cf.* § 4.2.9).

4.1.4. *Bridge*

A bridge links two buses together. It must respect their electrical and temporal specifications. A bridge can be as simple as a driver (signal amplifier), which isolates and amplifies the signals (buffering). This corresponds to the function of a repeater. Most of the time, it has its own RAM (Random Access Memory), which can be FIFO (First-In First-Out), or a Double Port DRAM (DP(DRA)M (Figure 4.8(b), *cf.* § 2.5.2 in Darche (2012)) so that the two buses can be kept functionally separate. This allows two elements belonging to different buses to be able to communicate, thus enabling retrocompatibility. An example of this is the ISA (Industry Standard Architecture) bus used in the original PC. In the 1990s, this bus coexisted alongside the PCI bus, which enabled a smooth transition for the computer industry in terms of input–output interface cards (Figure 4.10).

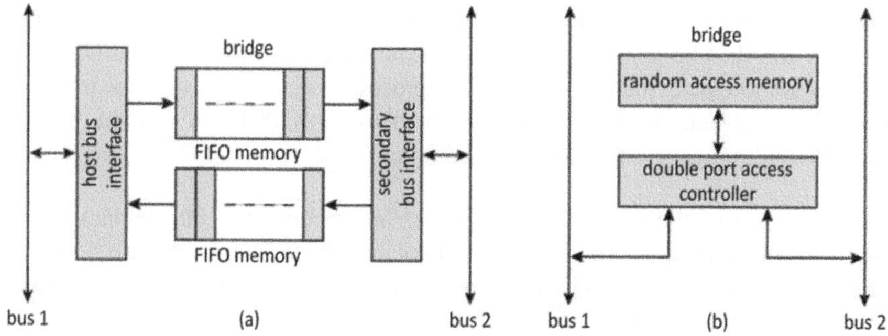

Figure 4.8. *Inter-bus communication through FIFO (a) and double port (b) memory devices*

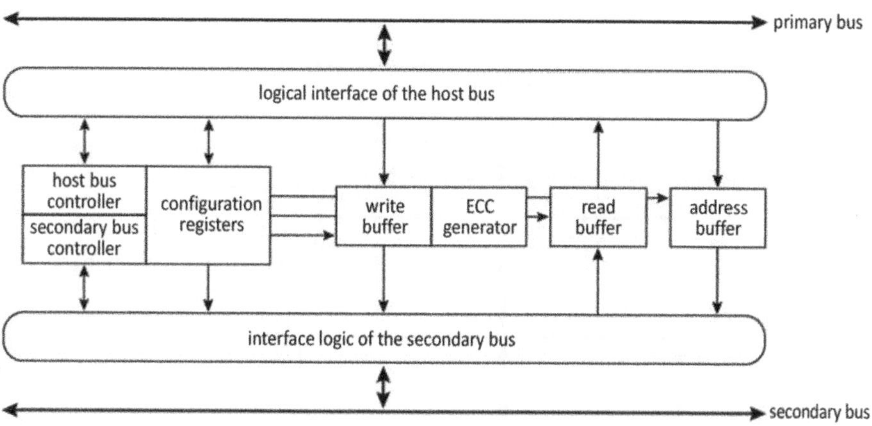

Figure 4.9. *A bus controller*

The greater the number of bus functionalities, the more complex the electronics. Bridges manage complex data paths. Simple electronic buffers are no longer adequate in this case, and a controller is required for each bus, as shown in Figure 4.9. In this example, the ability to initiate exchanges is only in the hands of a master of the first bus, which in this case is called the primary, or upstream, bus. The second bus is called the secondary, or downstream, bus. A bus controller can carry out simple operations on the data, such as address translation (*cf.* Childers and Baden (1997), for example), byte swapping, temporary storage (buffer or cache) of data or addresses (not shown), or complex processes such as the packing/unpacking of packets, or protocol translations. The management of interrupts and of DMAs must be taken into account. An Error-Detecting Circuit (EDC) or even Error Checking and Correcting (ECC) can be considered, based on logical parity, for example (*cf.* § III.6.6 in Darche (2000)). A codeword can thus be generated for the detection of errors on the fly, during a write phase. In some cases, such as with a multiprocessor system, an address translation must be carried out. A study of the bridge between a PCI bus and the bus of a MC68000 multiprocessor was done by Rodriguez Corral *et al.* (2002).

Examination of the elements of a modern microcomputer, but belonging to an older generation, reveals different types of interconnected buses (Figure 4.10). The local bus, which is implied to be local to the microprocessor, communicates with the north bridge. The memory bus is dedicated to the main – or primary – memory. The PCI and ISA expansion buses allow for the connection of I/O interface cards. The AGP (Accelerated Graphics Port) expansion card, which is one of the second-generation PC buses (*cf.* § 4.2.4), is dedicated to the display interface (*cf.* § 9.1 in Darche (2003)). The I/O bus is reserved for communication with devices.

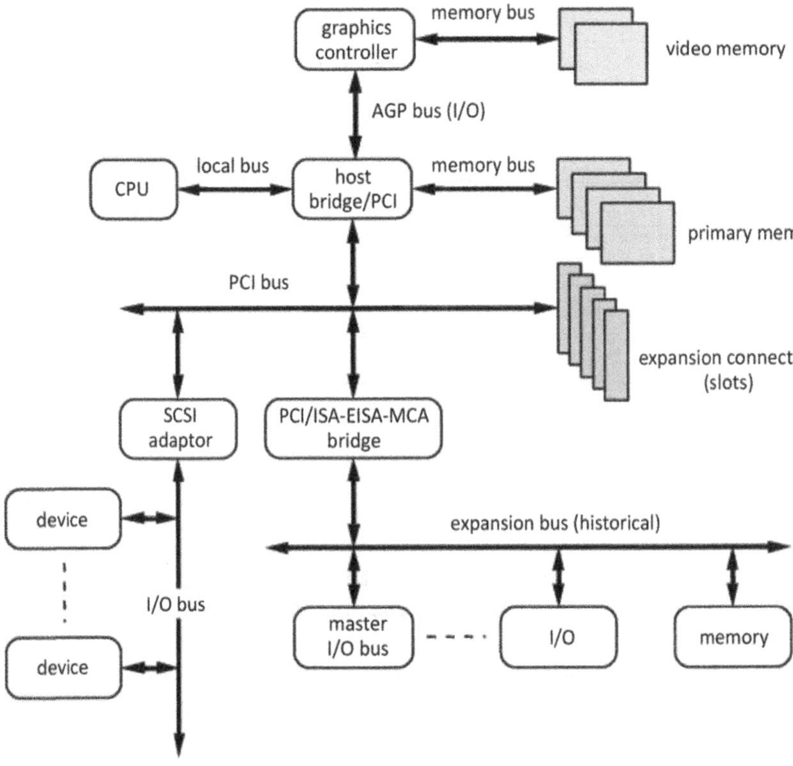

Figure 4.10. *Block diagram of a PC type microcomputer of the n-2 generation (1997)*

Based on this diagram, the bus can be categorized into six main families (Figure 4.11): local bus, link bus, memory bus, expansion bus (called "system bus" at Intel), I/O bus and backplane bus. The first five buses are used in (micro-)computers. The sixth is targeted more specifically at industrial real-time systems. On top of this, there is also the field bus, which is used in process control, as well as the power bus. The next section looks at these in more detail.

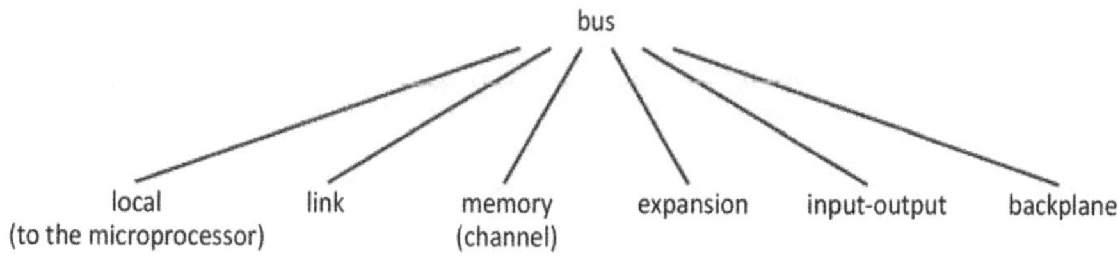

Figure 4.11. *Classification of buses by category*

4.2. Classification of digital system buses

This section aims to introduce buses that are presented in the industry depending on their location in a digital system.

4.2.1. *Local bus*

This is the lowest level, as it can be found at the component level. It is located on the Printed Circuit Board (PCB) itself. The local bus is the bus of the microprocessor, which is the sole initiator of exchanges, unless a DMA controller is present. The signals are those emanating from this initiator. In terms of PCs in particular, the examples include the VLB, BSB and FSB buses (Figure 4.12).

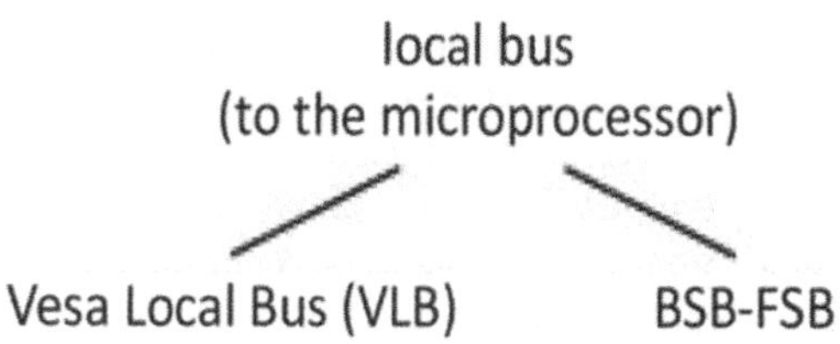

Figure 4.12. *The local bus*

Commercially speaking, the VESA (Video Electronics Standards Association) Local Bus (VLB), birthed from a consortium of companies, allowed the connection of one to three rapid controllers to the local bus, depending on the version (A or B). It preferentially addressed the display interface. This bus was an expansion of the bus of microprocessor 80486 made by the company Intel. Figure 4.13 shows its block diagram.

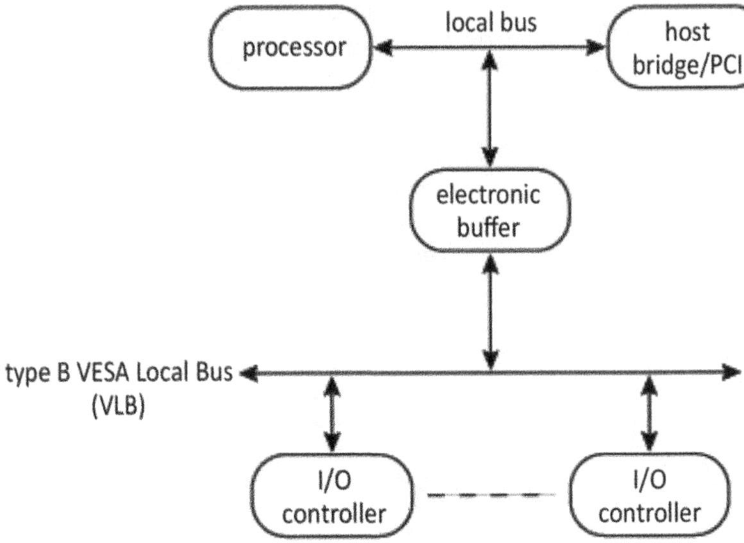

Figure 4.13. *Block diagram of the VL-Bus*

The architecture of the Dual Independent Buses (DIB) made by the company Intel in the middle of the 1990s for its Pentium Pro and II/III microprocessors allowed for separation of the cache traffic from the traffic of the main memory and of the I/O. The Back-Side Bus (BSB) made the CPU communicate with its external cache, while the Front-Side Bus (FSB) would communicate with the northbridge chipset, or the Graphics and Memory Controller Hub (GMCH), which comprised a graphics controller (Figure 4.14). Nowadays, the BSBs and the FSBs are integrated with the cache and the northbridge chipset into the MPU (MicroProcessor Unit). The I/O controllers are integrated into the southbridge chipset or the I/O Controller Hub (ICH). The role of the chipsets is explained in § V5-3.3.

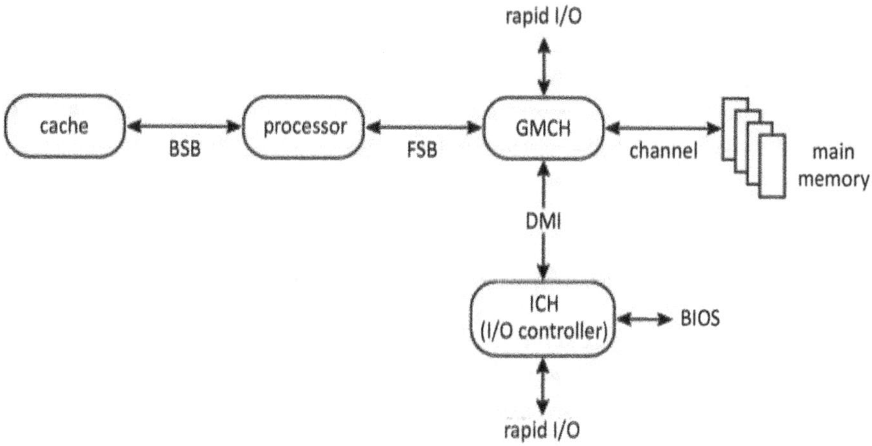

Figure 4.14. *Double independent bus (DIB) architecture*

Two older examples are the Z-bus (Zilog 1985) made by the company Zilog, which connected components of the Z800, Z8000 and Z80,000 families, and the Microbus, made by the company National Semiconductor (NS).

4.2.2. *Memory buses*

In the case of a system of memories, a controller serves several ranks or memory devices connected to each other via several channels or memory buses (Figure 4.15). By increasing the number of channels, an interleaving access can be established (*cf.* § 2.4.4 in Darche (2012)).

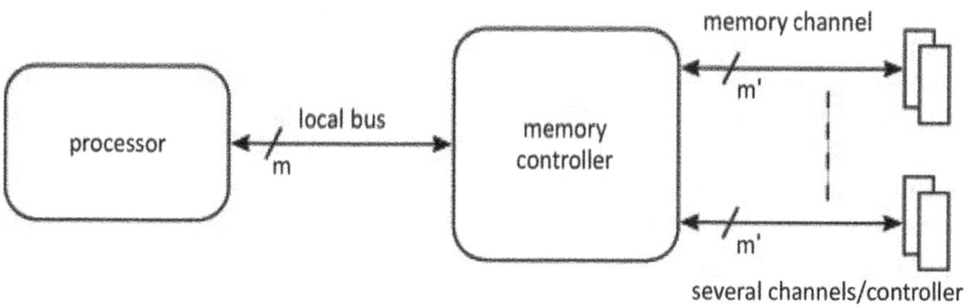

Figure 4.15. *The memory in its environment*

The channel is specific to a given family of memory devices. There is a return to the alternative forms of communication by cycle or by packet (Figure 4.16). A circuit like the IDT73720 from the company Integrated Device Technology, Inc. (IDT) enables two memory banks to be managed at the same time, with the possibility of having interleaved addressing, and thus doubling the bandwidth through burst access.

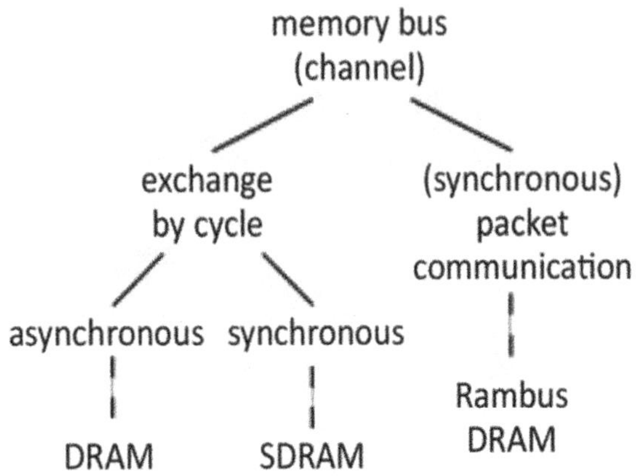

Figure 4.16. *Memory buses*

The bus present in cycle-based communication dynamic memory devices, as well as the memory channel of the Rambus memory using packet-based communication, has been examined in detail in § 5.2.3, 6.9 and 7.2.1 in Darche (2012).

4.2.3. *Link buses*

Link buses link microprocessors to each other or to a bridge. There are three principal link buses (Figure 4.17). They are characterized by a point-to-point link that carries rapid signals using technology based on differential low-voltage logic, such as the LVDS (Low-Voltage Differential (LVD) Signaling). Communication takes place through packets, the advantage here being the lack of cycles. A packet is the base element of communication, and a transaction is a sequence of packets. A transaction results in a transfer of information. One advantage of packet communication is that error detection – and even correction – can be added, as can flow control like in a network.

Figure 4.17. *A PC link bus (2013)*

The HyperTransport bus (HT), whose codename is "Lightning Data Transport" (LDT), was initiated by the company AMD, and enables a CPU to be connected to other CPUs or co-processors, to the memory and to other I/O controllers, southbridge chipset of the PC or interface cards. The base connection is a two-directional link, whose format of n varies from 2 to 32 bits, with a growth factor of 2. It has three signal families, which are CAD (Command, Address, Data), CTL (ConTroL) and CLK (CLocK), which are differential in nature (Figure 4.18). The format m of the CTL varies from 4 to 16 depending on the value of the format n.

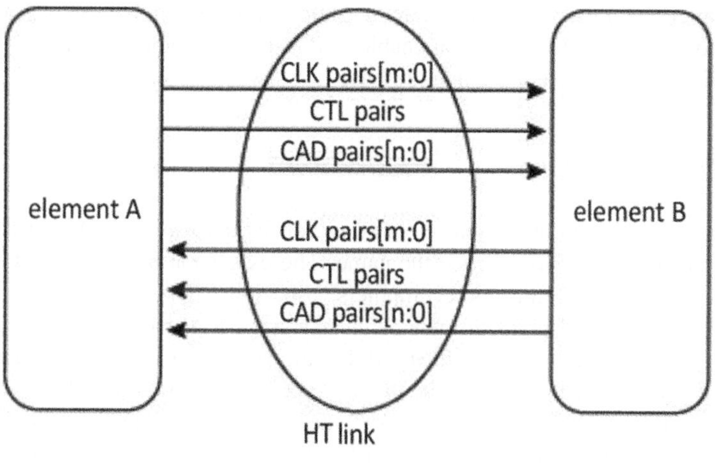

Figure 4.18. *HyperTransport type link*

The transfer is of the DDR type (Double Data Rate, *cf.* § 3.4 and 6.5 in Darche (2012)), with a clockspeed of 800 MHz in full-duplex, which results in a maximum bitrate of 1.6 Gb/s per link. Table 4.2 shows the values of the maximum bitrates depending on the version used. More information can be found in Trodden and Anderson (2003) and Holden *et al.* (2008).

Features	Versions			
	HT 1.x	HT 2.0	HT 3.0	HT 3.1
Year	2001	February 2004	April 2006	August 2008
Maximum frequency (GHz)	0.8	1.4	2.6	3.2
Max bitrate per 32-bit link (Gb/s)	12.8	256	41.6	51.2
Hot plugging	No	No	Yes	Yes

Table 4.2. *Binary outputs of the different versions of the HyperTransport bus*

Originally made by Intel (2004), the DMI bus (Direct Media Interface) links the northbridge chipset (MCH) to the southbridge one (ICH). As a reminder, the southbridge chipset is the loaded chip of the I/O. The bitrate is equal to 10 Gbit/s × 2 per link (type x4). Version 2.0, which came out in 2011, doubled the bitrate.

The QPI bus (Quick Path Interconnect, internally known as CSI for "Common System Interface") was released by Intel in 2008, following the HyperTransport, from which it drew a lot of inspiration. It enables CPUs to communicate with each other or with the ICH. The bus has a width of 20 bits.

4.2.4. *Expansion slot bus*

In an expansion slot bus, connectors allow for the insertion of I/O interface cards, also called expansion cards, hence the name. The expansion bus is the equivalent of the backplane bus but for microcomputers, especially IBM's PC. It was initially regarded from a signal point of view as an extension of the microprocessor bus. Its protocol is therefore heavily influenced by the latter's. In order to separate the microprocessor and memory from the I/O, an expansion bus was introduced that some manufacturers call the "system bus". The idea originally came from the company Apple, and was first seen in the Apple II (*cf.* § V5-3.1). The idea was next used by IBM in its personal computer (PC). This approach allows the I/O to be configured, and to later modify this configuration, while easily trouble-shooting the computer. It also frees up a significant amount of space as the third dimension can be used. Disadvantages include a limit on the number of connectors for electrical reasons and because of the space taken up on the printed circuit, issues to do with air flow stemming from the vertical arrangement of daughterboards, which can disturb the flow of cooling air, and the low reliability of slottable connectors. An electrical link can form between two adjacent daughterboards; an example of this is the

SLI (Scalable Link Interface), produced by the company Nvidia to link two graphics cards (Figure 4.19).

Figure 4.19. *The SLI by Nvidia. For a color version of this figure, see www.iste.co.uk/darche/microprocessor2.zip*

Figure 4.20 shows a classification. Initially, the bus was dedicated to a given microprocessor, or to a family of MPUs. This meant that the bus signals were actually the microprocessor signals amplified by electronic buffers. With the exception of the AGP bus, these constituted the first generation of PC buses. Nowadays, the expansion bus is independent from the MPU, thus enabling a vast array of choice of expansion cards. The PCI/PCI-X and the PCI Express make up the second and third generations respectively.

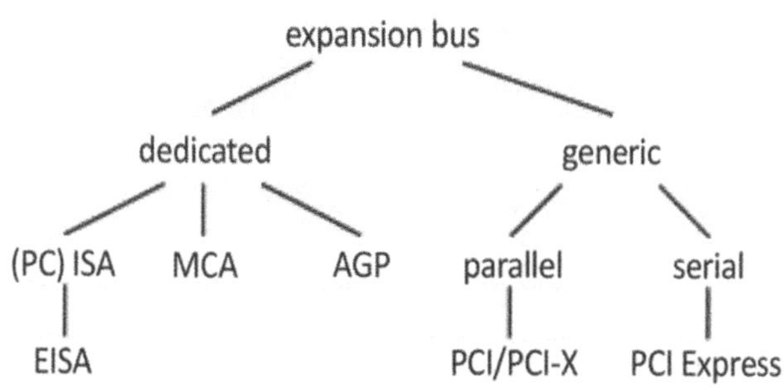

Figure 4.20. *Expansion bus of the PC and PS/2 microcomputers*

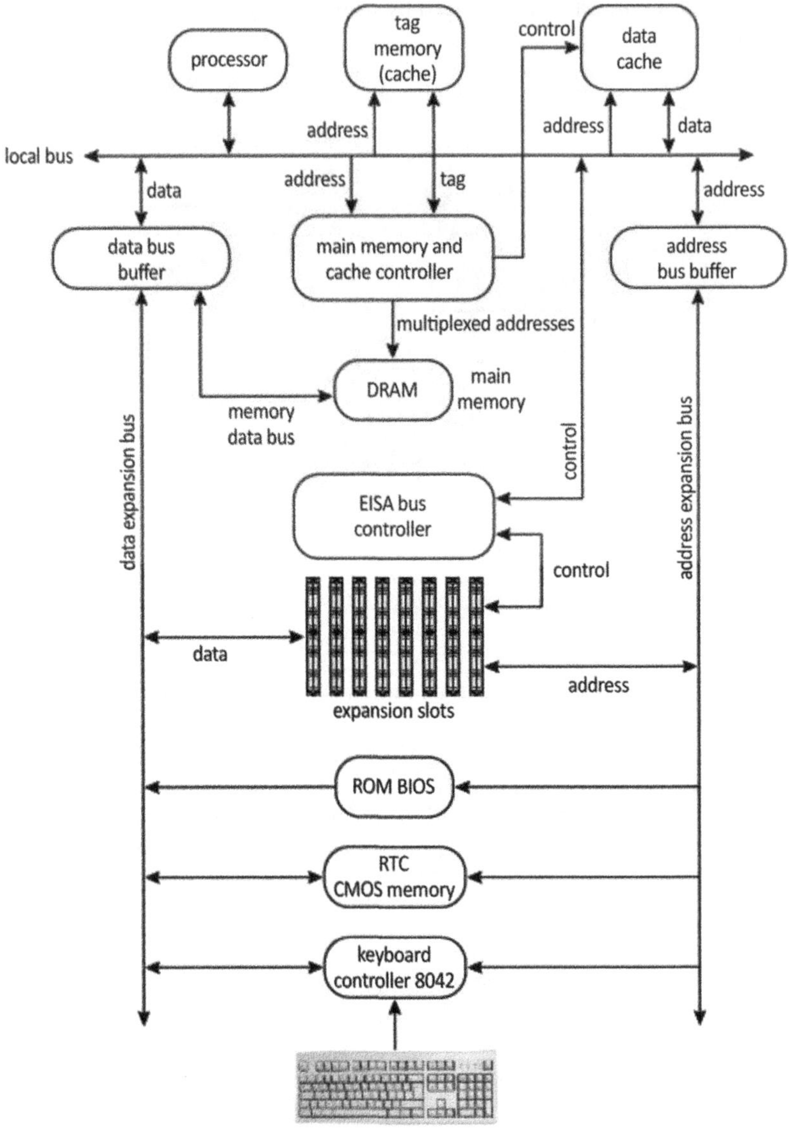

Figure 4.21. *Block diagram of an EISA system*

The PC bus could be found in the first ever PCs in 1981 (*cf.* § V5-3.2). It was made up of two rows of 31 signals mainly coming from the Intel 8088 microprocessor. The exchanges were clocked by the clock signal (Clk) at a frequency of 4.77 MHz. There was the address signals A[19:0], the data signals D[7:0], read and write memory signals (-MEMR and -MEMW), read and write I/O signals (-IOR and -IOW), as well as the management, interrupt (IRQ_0 to IRQ_7, Reset) and DMA signals. The electrical power was also present (±5 V and ±12 V). The width of the bus was then increased to 16 bits, with a frequency of 8 MHz. The XT and AT buses (Advanced Technology, *cf.* § V5-3.2.2) by IBM were next specified by the company Intel under the name "Industry Standard Architecture", or "ISA" (*cf.* Intel (1989) for version 2). Several works have covered the ISA, such as Solari (1994) and Shanley and Anderson (1995a). The 32-bit ISA compatible version was named EISA for "Extended ISA" (Figure 4.21). This specification was published in 1988, one year after the release of the first PC of the PS/2 range (Personal System/2). It was made available by the "Gang of Nine" (Compaq Computer Corp., AST Research Inc., Epson America Inc., Hewlett-Packard (HP), NEC Corp., Ing C. Olivetti & Co., Tandy Corp., Wyse Technology and Zenith Data Systems), a group made up of the nine leading companies in the market of PC clones (1/3 of the microcomputer market in 1987, compared to 26.8% for IBM) in response to the attempt by IBM to lock down the market of microcomputers by patenting its MCA bus (Micro Channel™ Architecture). More information on this bus can be found in Shanley and Anderson (1995b), among others. Chapter 8 provides examples of practical applications of this bus.

Table 4.3 presents the main characteristics of the buses found in these first PC type architectures.

The PCI bus is a project initiated by Intel in 1992, and whose reference document (PCI-SIG 1993a, 1993b) was published by a consortium of companies called the PCI-SIG (for PCI Special Interest Group), which grouped together all of the main actors of microcomputing, including Dell, IBM, Fujitsu, HP-Compaq, NEC, Microsoft and Western Digital. The PCI bus was designed to fulfill the need for a high-speed expansion bus and, most importantly, one that was independent from the processor. The interface electronics of the bus thus only rely on the bus signals, and no longer on those of the entities connected to the bus. As a result, a manufacturer can sell the same I/O interface for different computers – a PC or a MacIntosh, for example. The difference is then only made by the driver (*cf.* § 4.2.2 in Darche (2003)) of the operating system. This bus is derived from the μP i486 bus, which is a multiplexed address/data bus with a width of 32 bits, and later 64 bits. Several PCI buses can be connected in a tree layout. An even logical parity control is established on the address and on the data. It presents a clock frequency that varies from continuous to 133.3 MHz. The advantage of a frequency of zero is the ability to halt the operation of a synchronous component, in order to reduce energy consumption, for example. At maximum frequency, the theoretical maximum transfer rate is 533 Mb/s for a bus width of 64 bits. The expansion connector in the 5 V version has four rows of 31 pins. The latest version is version 3.0 (PCI-SIG 2002). It was described in detail in Shanley and Anderson (1995c) and Weiss and Finkelstein (1999).

Type	PC	ISA	EISA	MCA
Generation	1st			
Width of the data bus (bits)	8	16	32	16/32
Width of the address bus (bits)	20	24	32	24/32
Address/data multiplexing	No	No	No	No
Clock (MHz)	4.77	8.33	8.33	10
Minimum number of cycles	2	2	1	1
Unit transfer bitrate (Mo/s)	24	8.33	16.66	13.11
Burst transfer bitrate (Mo/s)	-	-	33.33	21.05
Multi-master	No	Yes (limited)	Yes	Yes
Notes	Original PC bus	16-bit AT PC bus	Retrocompatibility with the ISA bus	PS/2 bus

Table 4.3. *Main features of the PC family buses (1/2)*

Released by Intel in 2004, the PCI Express (acronym: PCI-E) belongs to the third generation of expansion buses for PC. It succeeds the PCI bus and the local AGP bus. With the impending arrival of version 5.0 (2019), it ensures ascending logical compatibility (*cf.* § V4-3.3.3) with the PCI bus at the level of the software drivers (*cf.* § 4.2.2 in Darche (2003)). The communication type is a bidirectional differential serial link in point-to-point full-duplex (i.e. between two cards), called "lane". The bitrate is currently doubling every 3 years. It can be modulated by increasing the number of links (x1, x2, x4, x8, x16 and x32) in order to reach the maximum of 32 GTransfers/s (version 5.0). A full description can be found in Budruk *et al.* (2003) and Jackson and Budruk (2012).

Table 4.4 summarizes the key features of these buses, which were the successors of the first PC buses. For a detailed comparison of these buses, see Finkelstein and Weiss (1999).

Type	PCI	PCI-E
Generation	2nd	3rd
Width of the data bus (bits)	32/64	Bidirectional serial link 1 (x1), 2 (×2), 4 (×4), 8 (×8), 16 (×16) and 32 (×32)
Width of the address bus (bits)	32/64	
Address/data multiplexing	Yes	-
Clock (MHz)	0 to 33, 66 or 133	2.5/5/8 GHz
Minimum number of cycles	1	-
Unit transfer bitrate (Mb/s)	33.33	≈ 4 Gb/s
Burst transfer bitrate (Mb/s)	132/264/533	32 GTransfers/s
Multi-master	Yes	Yes
Notes	Father of the PCI-E	Current PC bus 8b/10b and 128b/130b codings

Table 4.4. *Main features of the PC family buses (2/2)*

4.2.5. *Expansion buses*

These buses enable a microprocessor board (a "baseboard") to have its own small I/O expansion board. It is therefore a board-level bus. A commercial example of this is the iSBX™ bus, part of the Multibus made by Intel, which gave rise to IEEE standard P959 (IEEE 1984). This document defines two formats for the cards: single or double wide. It supports interrupt and transfer requests such as the DMA.

4.2.6. *I/O buses*

An I/O bus links one or more devices to one or several I/O controllers. An I/O bus can depend on a group of devices (e.g. for the interfaces of mass storage units ATA (AT Attachment, *cf.* § 9.2.3 in Darche (2003)), in the parallel version (PATA for Parallel ATA), or in series (SATA for Serial ATA), or it can be generic (e.g. the SCSI (Small Computer System Interface, *cf.* § 9.3.1 in Darche (2003)). Figure 4.22 presents those most commonly found in a PC. It should be noted that for the USB (Universal Serial Bus), this a logical bus, as opposed to a physical bus, in the sense that the host controller directly communicates with the devices, and that the bandwidth is shared. The connection between devices is a point-to-point connection, and it has a tiered star topology. This looks like a tree where the leaves are the devices.

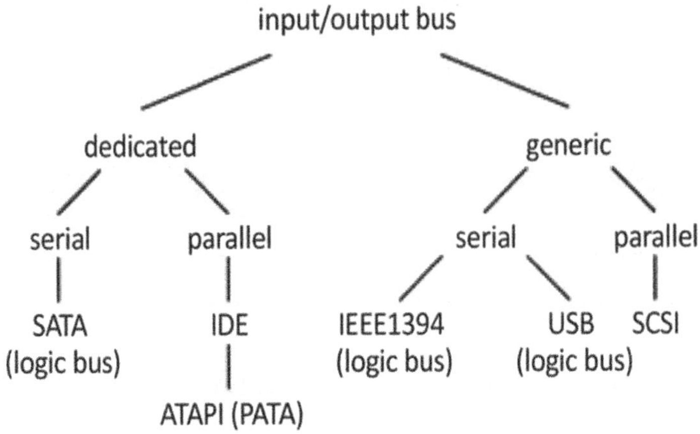

Figure 4.22. *The I/O buses*

4.2.7. *Backplane and centerplane buses*

A backplane bus enables communication between connected electronic cards (backplane interface). It is the printed circuit board (motherboard[1]) version of the ribbon cable. Parallel copper traces (for parallel transmission) or serial traces link the slot connectors (or card-edge connectors) so that the daughterboards can be slotted in. Guiding rails are placed at each extremity of the connectors in order to center the electronic board. A locking system can be set up so as to avoid the possibility of pull-out occurring (Figure 4.23); screws can also be fixed onto the front face for the same purpose. Good reliability at high bitrates is an advantage of this type of bus.

1 This term should not be confused with the equipped printed circuit used in a microcomputer.

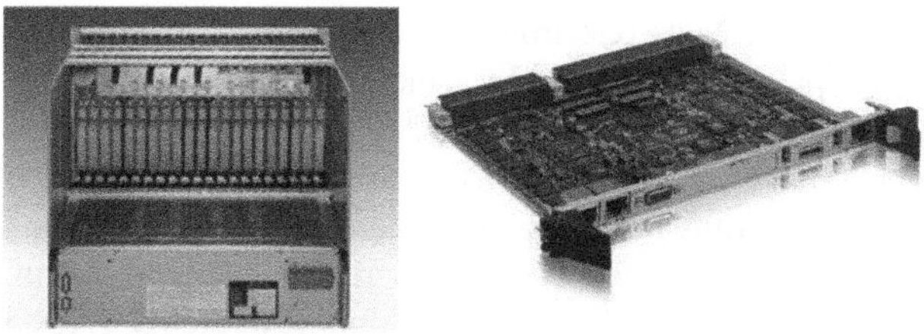

Figure 4.23. *A VME64x chassis with its backplane and a VPX 6U board. For a color version of this figure, see www.iste.co.uk/darche/microprocessor2.zip*

The PCB of the daughterboard can also serve as a male connector: it is split in such a way that the traces of the PCB (direct-edge connector) come into contact with the contacts of the female card-edge connector by insertion. This approach is sensitive to attacks from the environment (abrasions, dust, changes in temperature, etc.). Corrosion can be avoided by using a gold coating on the surface, but this can be worn down through repeated abrasion during the slotting/removal of the electronic card. An alternative to this solution is an indirect, or "two-part", connection. In such a case, the daughterboard can have a male connector in lieu of the traces. The advantage of having a male connector instead of the contact points of the daughterboard's printed circuit is the possibility of having more than two rows of contacts, and higher levels of reliability thanks to greater protection of these contact points. An example of an indirect connector for a standardized bus is the EURODIN DIN41612 (IEC 60603-2) connector, which is shown in Figure 4.24.

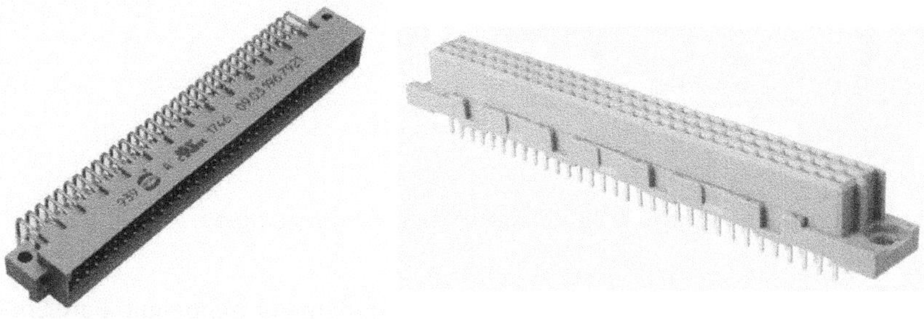

Figure 4.24. *Female and male connectors, standard DIN41612. For a color version of this figure, see www.iste.co.uk/darche/microprocessor2.zip*

The bus locations are usually unimportant, meaning that a daughterboard can be slotted into any connector. This bus removes the need for cabling with electrical wires, and therefore the presence of cabling errors and inherent failures. It provides mechanical support in the case of these occurring. The density of the daughterboard is maximal. It facilitates reuse and interoperability, all the more so if the bus is standardized. Connection costs (electronic, electrical and mechanical costs) are also reduced. This principal has been reused for the expansion buses of the motherboard (*cf.* § 4.2.4). The electrical power supply is also provided through a power bus with wide, thick copper traces along which the current can pass (order of magnitude: usually several dozen Amperes (A)). An example of a backplane bus was the OMNIBUS® made by the company DEC; a description can be found in DEC (1970). In the field of microcomputers, we can cite the example of the ALTAIR 8800 (Roberts and Yates 1975a b) made by the American company MITS (*cf.* § V1-1.2).

If the bus is active, line drivers condition the signals. If required by the exchange type, a clock does the clocking. Line terminations, whether active or passive, can also be installed. An electrical link can exist between a daughterboard and another backplane bus.

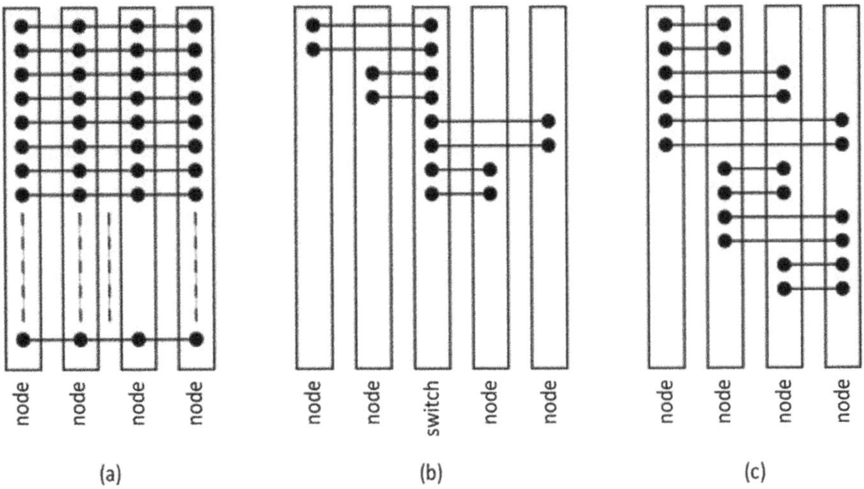

Figure 4.25. *Classical backplane topologies*

The backplane connection can be either point-to-point or multipoint. Furthermore, it can be either a serial link (bit-to-bit) or a parallel one. Figure 4.25(a) presents the classical bus communication. The serial version has two types of architecture, the star type (Figure 4.25(b)) and the mesh type (Figure 4.25(c)). Case b uses a crossbar switch. This is an effective solution, which tends to be used in network equipment. An associated piece of technology is the "switch fabric".

In order to minimize the distances between connectors, and therefore to decrease the total length of the bus, the "centerplane" bus version was developed. It involves placing the connectors throughout the printed circuit board, as shown in Figure 4.26.

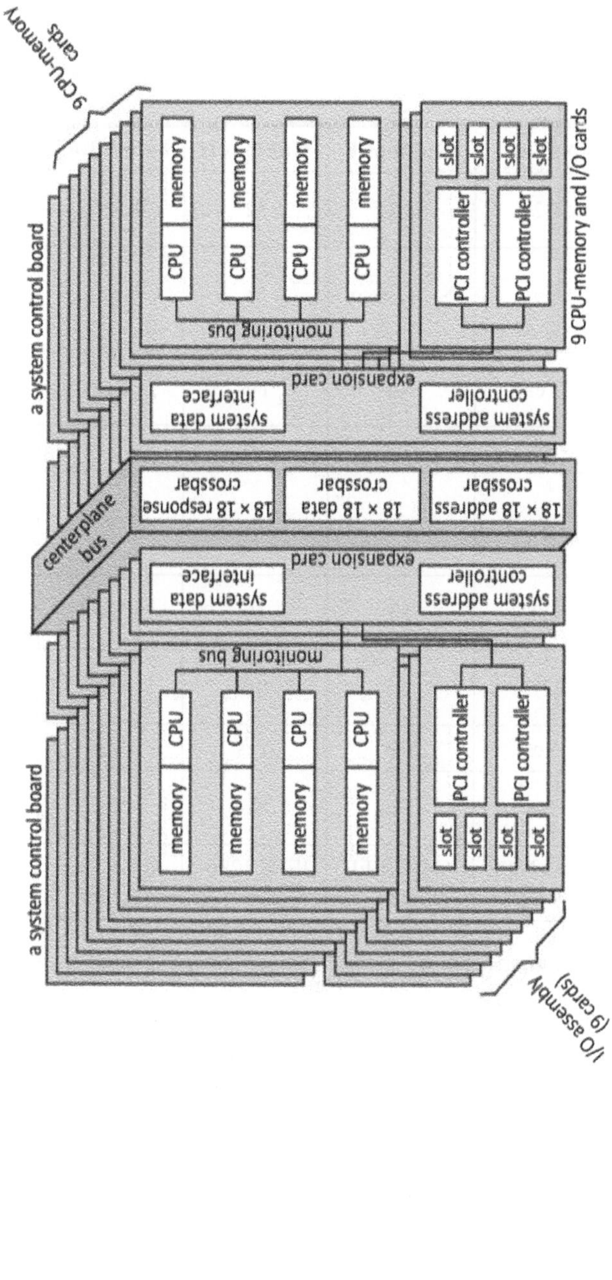

Figure 4.26. *An example of a centerplane bus, inspired by the Sun Fire™ E25K/E20K systems (2006)*

Connections tend to become point-to-point in order to provide ever-increasing bitrates. Techniques taken from wired and optical networks have been used, such as in the 8/10-bit and 64/66-bit SONET (Synchronous Optical NETwork) encoding schemes, which is what the consortium of companies HSBI (High-Speed Backplane Initiative, created in 2002) uses. SONET provides a point-to-point communication link via a backplane bus, with a minimum bitrate of 4.976 Gb/s, and a peak bitrate of 6.375 Gb/s, over a distance of 75 cm. In 2003, it merged with the OIF (Optical Internetworking Forum).

Type	NuBus	Multibus I	Multibus II	FutureBus+	VME
Width of data bus (bits)	32	16	32	32/256	16/64
Width of address bus (bits)	32	24 (16 I/O)	32	32/64	24/64
Address/data multiplexing	Yes	No	Yes	Yes	Yes/no
Clock (MHz)	10	5	10	-	-
Minimum number of cycles	2	-	1	-	-
Unit transfer bitrate (Mo/s)	20	10	40	200	40
Burst transfer bitrate (Mo/s)	37.5	-	40	4000	80
Multi-master	Yes	Yes	Yes	Yes	Yes
Split transaction	No	No	No	Yes	No
Standard	ANSI/IEEE 1196-1987	ANSI/IEEE 796	IEEE 1296-1987	IEEE 896. 1-1987	IEEE 1014-1987

Table 4.5. *Main features of the representative backplane buses*

Two commercial examples are the VME bus (Versa Module European) and the VPX bus (VITA 46). The former is an open parallel commercial bus standard. It dominated real-time industrial systems and was described by DeBock (1982). VMEbus is the standardized version, under ANSI/IEEE standard 1014-1987 (IEEE 1987). The second example, also called VITA (VMEbus International Trade Association) 46, is its successor, going from a parallel version to a modern serial version. Introduced in 2007, it was designed to support different buses like the Serial RapidIO®, PCIe, SATA, gigabit Ethernet, etc. Table 4.5 shows a reminder of their main features, comparing them to other common buses. In the early 2010s, backplane connectors provided a maximum bitrate of 5, 10 and 25 Gb/s, marginally[2] 40 Gb/s for a characteristic impedance of 85, 100 or, more rarely, 50 Ω. The commercial backplane buses are described in Di Giacomo (1990). VME64 is a 64-bit version, standardized under reference ANSI/VITA 1-1994.

4.2.8. *Fieldbus*

The fieldbus goes a bit beyond the scope of this chapter. In reality, it is closer to a network of a defined area, which could be an automobile or a production unit. The element that is most often associated with the fieldbus is the "Programmable Logic Controller" (PLC). It interacts with the bus through measurement instruments, sensors and actuators. The term "fieldbus" is used in opposition to the term "computer bus". The fieldbus does indeed tend to be a lot simpler, due to the small amount of digital resources included inside industrial sensors and actuators. It is also more resilient when faced with external disturbances, as it must be able to operate even in very noisy environments (industrial environments). Another key element regarding fieldbuses is their deterministic and real-time aspects. Examples of industrial products are the serial CAN (Controller Area Network) bus, produced in 1983 by the company Bosch for the automobile industry, and standardized by ISO (International Organization for Standardization) in 1986 under the standard ISO 11898, Profibus/Profinet, and the Interbus made by Phoenix Contact. There is also the VAN (Vehicle Area Network), first heralded by the automobile companies PSA (*Peugeot Société Anonyme*) and Renault.

4.2.9. *SoC: from bus to network*

A SoC (System on (a) Chip, *cf.* § V1-1.2) is the result of an integration of components from the system level (i.e. microprocessors, memories and I/O controllers) down to the level of a single chip. Originally, the architecture of communication between internal function blocks was specific (called "custom" or "ad hoc"), and point-to-point in nature. Starting in 1995, the external buses of the microprocessor, as well as their protocols, became integrated (called "on-chip bus", as opposed to the

2 The company FCI announced in January 2015 that it had achieved a transfer along a backplane bus of 56 Gb/s without any errors, using duobinary encoding (EDN January 30, 2015).

"off-chip bus"). In this way, a SoC bus carries out the same functions as the external buses, but at the level of a chip. There have been buses within this component since the advent of the very first microprocessor in 1971, but these were all *ad hoc* solutions. The shared bus structure has been adapted to systems with low numbers of components, as it does not survive the change in scale. A SoC can integrate several dozen components to be interconnected. The bus has therefore been adapted as an external element in the Single Shared Bus (SSB, Figure 4.27(a)) version, in the split-bus structure (Figure 4.27(b)), in the hierarchical bus structure (Figure 4.27(c)) and in the multiple bus structure (Figure 4.27(d)). Each node is a Processing Element – or Unit (PE or PU), made up of a processor P and of its local memory M, and which is connected to the bus through a functional subset called a "wrapper" (W). Depending on the direction of the communication, access to the bus is ensured through classical buffers, or through three-state output transceivers, if required. The communication element between two buses is either simply a transceiver (Figure 4.27(b)) or, in more advanced cases, a bridge (Figure 4.27(c)), hence the acronym HBB, for Hierarchical Bus Bridge (architecture). An example of this is the ASB bus with the AMBA (Arm® Microcontroller Bus Architecture) specification, from the company Arm® Ltd (originally Acorn RISC Machine, and later Advanced RISC Machines). Remember that this hierarchization (*cf.* § 4.1.2) increases the bitrate (compared to the single version) by isolating the nodes by their bitrate class. The electrical load of the bus is therefore decreased. The transactions can take place in parallel along each bus. Moreover, in order to save on energy, a local bus can be put on standby (Zhang *et al.* 1998; Chen *et al.* 1999).

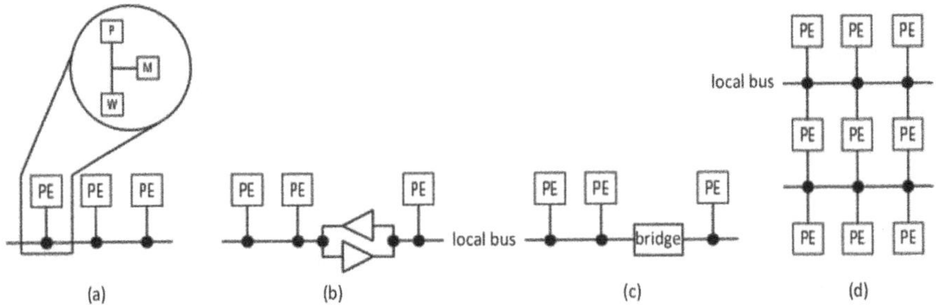

Figure 4.27. *Variations on the concept of a shared bus*

An alternative to the shared version of the bus is the AND-OR bus, as shown in Figure 4.38(a). Another approach is the multiplexer-based bus. Figure 4.28(b) illustrates an example.

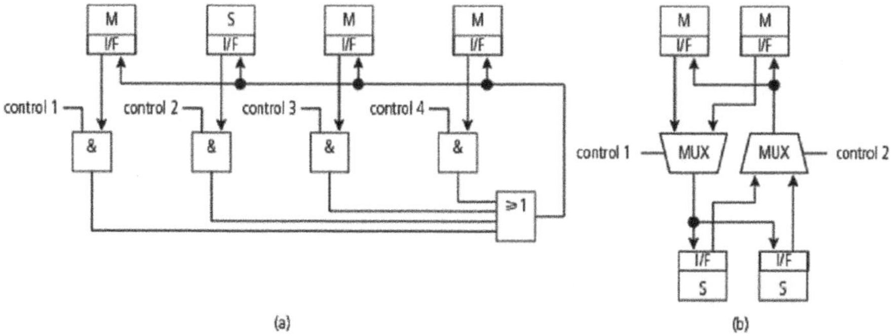

Figure 4.28. *AND–OR bus and multiplexer-based bus*

We can cite other representative industrial examples, such as the CoreConnect Bus Architecture from IBM, whose bus topology and standard are free, the open-source bus WISHBONE (WISHBONE SoC Interconnection Architecture) (OpenCores 2010), as well as the Split Transaction Bus (STBus®), made by the company STMicroelectronics. For the latter, one of its instantiations is the bus matrix with the crossbar (i.e. a switch matrix), which can be either partial (Figure 4.29(a)) or whole (Figure 4.29(b)); the latter is also called the point-to-point bus architecture.

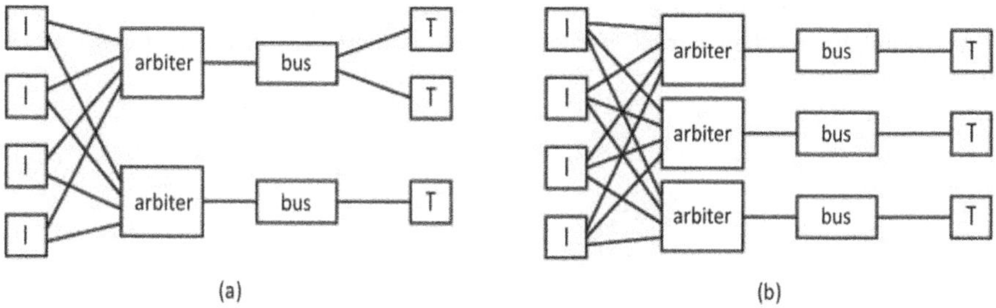

Figure 4.29. *Bus matrices: partial (a) and complete (b)*

From the 2000s onwards, SoCs have acquired multiple masters, and, most of the time, they have multiple, heteregeneous (i.e. different) processors (MPSoC, or "MultiProcessor SoC"). While bus-based topologies tend to be widespread in the area of SoC for historical reasons, they present some major disadvantages, such as high levels of energy consumption, and poor scalability, if any at all. Other topologies, notably from the field of networks and from parallel computer architectures, have been suggested with their protocols. Among these static, direct connection (i.e. point-to-point) topologies, there is the linear array (Figure 4.30(a)), the ring (Figure 4.30(b)), with a possible variation being the counter-rotating ring, also called the double ring, and the slightly more complex cordal ring (Figure 4.30(c)). The cordal ring is a fully connected network. Each PE is connected to a communication element of the network that carries out the functions of connection or of routing (Router Element, or Router Unit (RE or RU)).

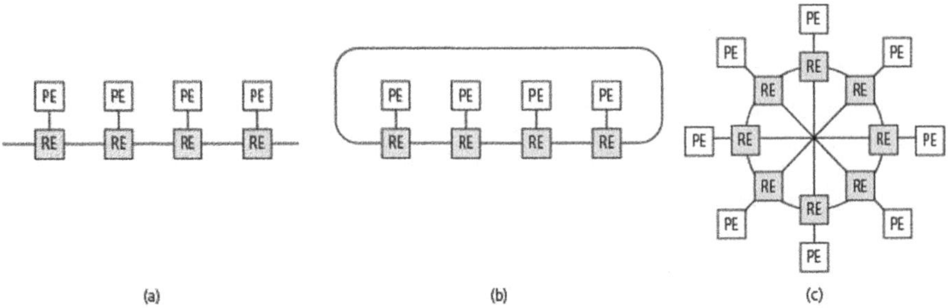

Figure 4.30. *Static interconnection network*

Even more complex, there is the crossbar switch (not shown here), the near-neighbor mesh (Figure 4.31(a)) or the unfolded torus (Figure 4.31(b)). The near-neighbor mesh is also called a 2D array. Note the feedback of the frontal nodes of the torus. A variation of the torus is the folded torus (Figure 4.31(c)), which is characterized by a constant distance between each of the nodes. The advantage of these topologies is their simple wiring, as well as their predictable features (bitrate, etc.).

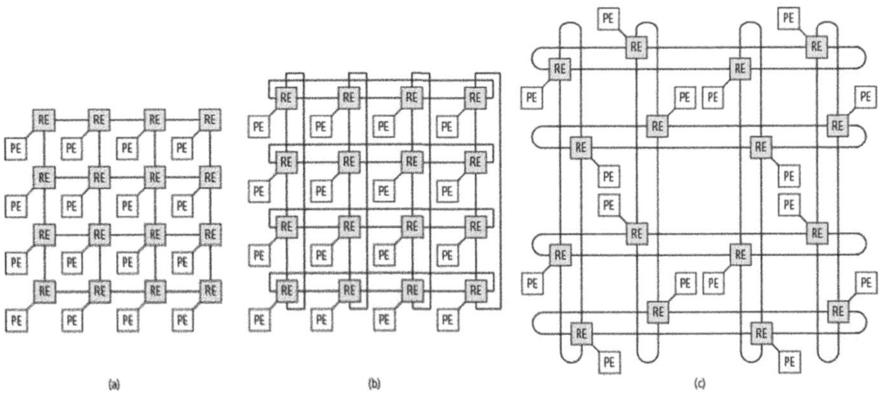

Figure 4.31. *Examples of different topologies: near-neighbor mesh (a), unfolded torus (b) and folded torus (c)*

Others are more complex, like the classical binary tree, shown in its balanced version in Figure 4.32(a), and in the fat-tree version (Leiserson 1985), where the bandwidth is greater toward the root, the cube (Figure 4.32(b)), or the 4D hypercube (four dimensions, i.e. a cube in a cube, not shown here). For the tree, each node is a switch. The leaves are PEs. This is therefore an indirect network.

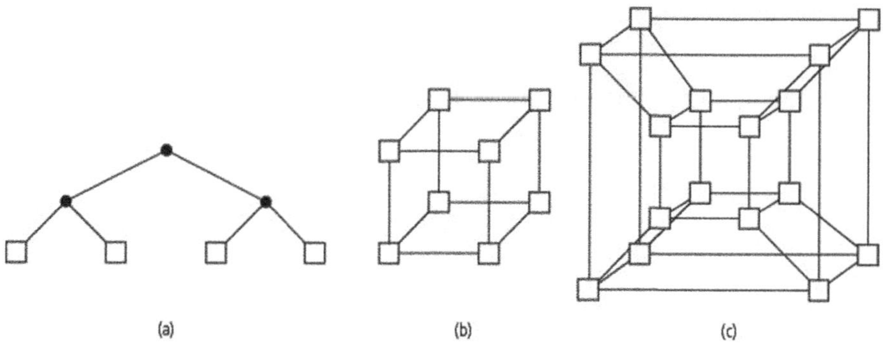

Figure 4.32. *Interconnection networks: indirect (a) and direct (b and c)*

Another form of indirect network with a dynamic connection is the butterfly network. It allows any node to be connected via several levels of switches, shown in grey in Figure 4.33.

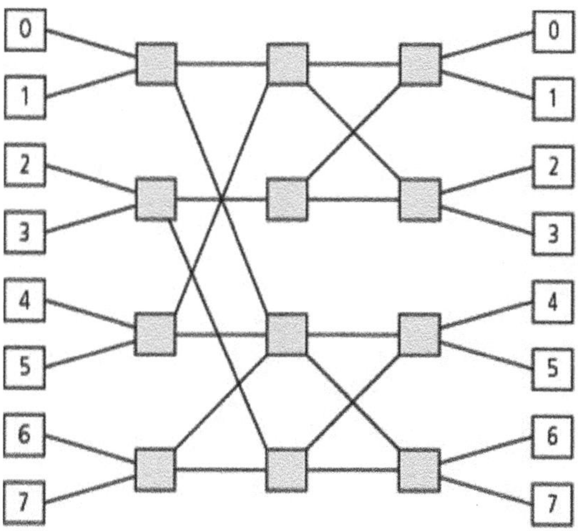

Figure 4.33. *Connections by a butterfly network*

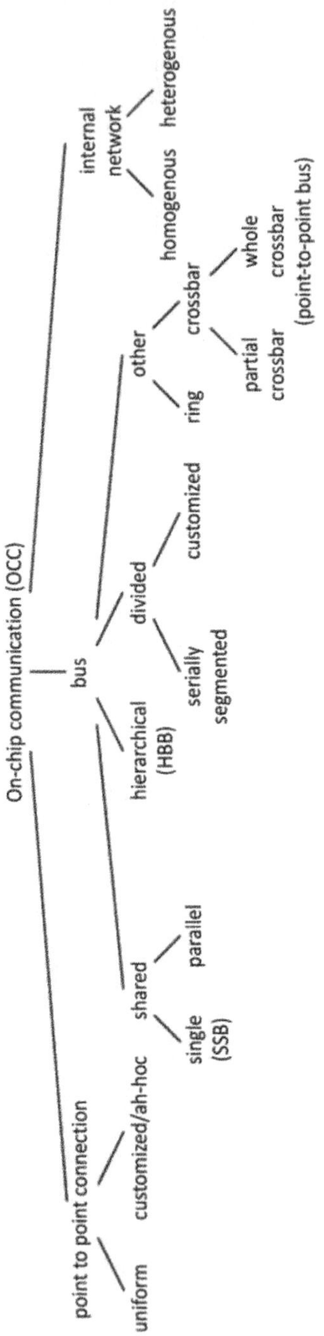

Figure 4.34. *Classification of on-chip internal architectures*

In order to achieve high-performance communication, the internal buses of these SoCs are in possession of the most advanced technical features, such as bus reservation, overlapped arbitration, the overlapping of data and address phases with out-of-order processing (*cf.* § 2.1.2). CoreConnect, for example, have all of these. They also tend to provide diffusion. Moreover, several provide packet-based communication, which is a technique that has its origins in computer networks, but which has been adapted to SoCs. These networks are called NoC[3] (Network-on-Chip). The move to networks is a normal evolution for the bus, providing a flexible solution in terms of scalability. There are two categories, which are circuit-switching networks and packet-switching networks. In a packet-switching network, there is no dedicated circuit and therefore no added costs associated with establishing a new circuit. The packet is the atomic unit of communication. It has a heading, which contains the routing information (source address and destination address, among others). The advantage of packet-based communication is that the packets can follow different paths in a multipath network. The order of reception can be different from the order of emission, and therefore a re-ordering mechanism must be put in place. AMBA-AHB uses split transactions. Using a network with packets means that the electrical characteristics can be predicted. The interface is standardized, which facilitates interconnection and allows components to be reused, which reduces costs. This type of network tends to be more extendible and more flexible. A disadvantage, however, is that the interface provided can have characteristics that are overly powerful for their intended use. Dally and Towles (2001) have covered these issues. Figure 4.34 shows a summary of the internal topologies (On-Chip Connection (OCC)) of all of the architectures presented. Their study goes beyond the scope of this work; they are dealt with exhaustively in Pasricha and Dutt (2008).

4.2.10. *Power bus*

Supplying power to a computer system is a complex process. It requires several different voltages (e.g. +3.3 V, +5 V and +12 V) that need to be precise (±5%, for example). These classical values for the voltage are tied to the technology of the logics used, or to particular components (e.g. the motors of the Hard Disk Drive or HDD). Nowadays, with the drive for integration, some ULSI components (Ultra Large Scale Integration, *cf.* § V1-1.2) like an MPU, a chipset or an FPGA (Field-Programmable Gate Array) require several different supply voltages for the core and the interface logic, as well as for other entities. Some sit at approximately 1 volt, with current surges of several dozen Amperes (30–50 A). The subset tasked with the power supply often has to respond to criteria that are contradictory in nature. For example, a high current delivered with a small drop in serial voltage, a short response time at high

3 More information in Gebali *et al.* (2009).

current surges, a precise regulation of the load variation and, or, lastly, a long line with a small value of the impedance.

In order to distribute these voltages, the power bus is made up of electrical supply lines and ground lines. As such, it is not a communication bus. The conductors (copper traces or wires) are very large and thick, in order to best carry strong currents and to limit any overly large drops in voltage. Decoupling capacitors can be distributed uniformly throughout in order to reduce the impedance of the supply lines, and thus to smooth out the voltage during current surges.

A power supply fulfills three many functions, which are electrical isolation, transformation (lowering, as well as raising the voltage) and controlling the voltage and the current. It has to isolate the input and the output for electrical (e.g. AC (Alternating Current) input and DC (Direct Current) output, different values of the voltage, etc.) as well as safety reasons. It transforms the input voltage into another voltage that is higher or lower. Lastly, the output voltage has to be precise (typical order of magnitude is 1–5%) for the powered electronics.

The power subset has changed over time with the technological advancement of electronic components and architectures (i.e. linear regulator followed by switching regulator). There are three classical architectures, which are the centralized power system, the distributed power system and the factorized power system, with the latter being the current approach.

Historically, the power supply architecture has been the centralized version, called CPA for Centralized Power (supply) Architecture. This is shown in Figure 4.35. A single converter delivers n regulated voltages under high currents over long distances, sometimes in the order of the meter. The power source has to be close to the AC entry point, for reasons of safety and of ElectroMagnetic Interference (EMI), meaning far away from the cards of the bus. Drops in voltage that go beyond a volt can then be seen at the end of the backplane bus as a result of the impedance of the lines, which implies high levels of power dissipation ($I^2 \times R$). Given that the source of the power is located in a single spot, cooling can be challenging, and the response time to load variations is high. Another major inconvenience is its lack of flexibility, as the number of distributed voltages cannot be extended, nor can the maximum current be changed. To add a voltage, a regulator would have to be added to the card itself. Because of these limitations, this type of power supply can still be found in low and medium power systems.

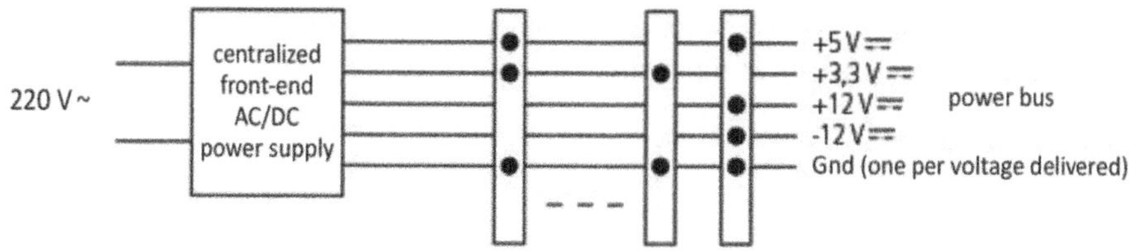

Figure 4.35. *Architecture of a centralized power supply*

In the 1970s, the PDE (Power Distribution Element) was invented, providing a great help to PCB designers. This was an insulated copper bar that was positioned vertically like a classical electronic component. The objective was to improve the component density and the electrical properties of the power bus. Carey and Grossman (1977) describe the principle and its use.

As a result of the high levels and variability of the currents causing voltage drops not tolerated by the electronics, and to reduce and distribute the overall thermal dissipation, at the end of the 1980s, the proposal was made to separate the central power supply into several modules for processing energy called "Power Processing Units" (PPUs). This type of system is called a "Distributed Power System" (DPS), or "Distributed Power Architecture" (DPA). The two main topologies are a series (or cascade) circuit (Figure 4.36(a)), and, for stronger currents, a parallel circuit (Figure 4.36(b)). Organization as a cascade helps optimize the various abovementioned functions of a power supply, with each module taking control of one of these. Parallel organization is beneficial in terms of the reliability of the global power supply system, as it provides redundancy and ease of maintenance, as well as allows for hot swapping. The advantages of this modularity are the standardization of the modules (electronic characteristics and encapsulation), which speeds up and simplifies design, ease of maintenance, and optimizes conversion yield and reliability by decreasing electrical and heat stresses.

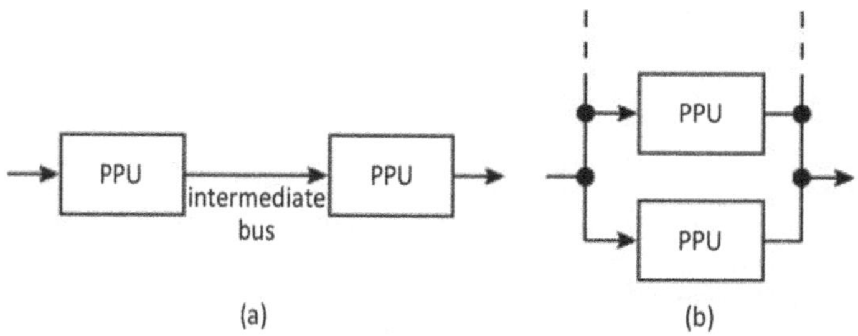

Figure 4.36. *Layout topologies of the PPUs in a cascade circuit (a) and a parallel circuit (b) (from Tabisz et al. (1992))*

In order to obtain different voltages, the modules can be stacked, either as additive stacking (Figure 4.37(a)) or as subtractive stacking (Figure 4.37(b)).

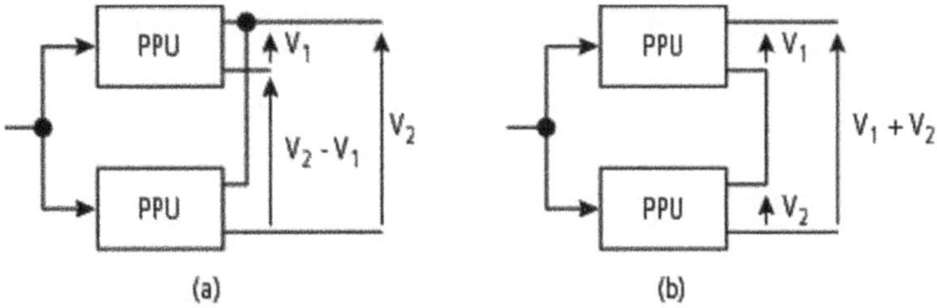

Figure 4.37. *Layout topologies of the PPUs in additive stacks (a) or subtractive stacks (b)*

Using this approach, it is possible to have several power sources ("source splitting", Figure 4.38(a)), or to provide several load points ("load splitting", Figure 4.38(b)). By allowing for several sources, an uninterrupted power supply system by battery can be created. The second option allows the supply to power electronic subsets located in different areas (distributed loads). In this way, regulation can be optimized, and the noise can be reduced. Adding an extra output voltage really means adding a simple output regulator, which affords a great amount of flexibility to the design. In this case, it is referred to as a modular power system.

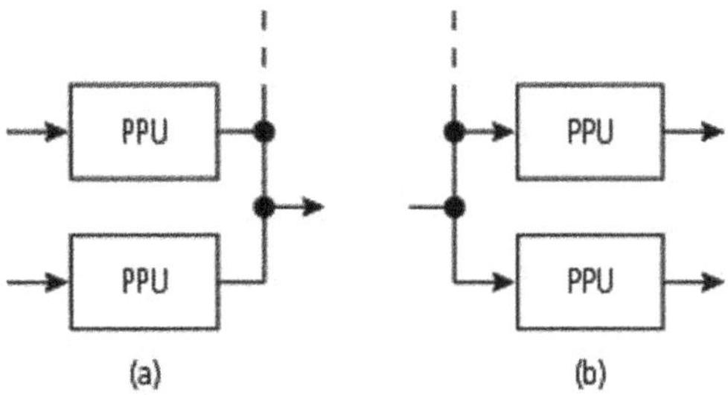

Figure 4.38. *Structure with source splitting and load splitting (from Tabisz et al. (1992))*

One such architecture is the one shown in Figure 4.39. A single weakly regulated voltage coming from the front-end converter is distributed by the backplane bus at a value of typically 48 V, which is a classic voltage used in the field of telecommunications. Non-isolated local voltage regulators, which are usually DC/DC converters, then provide the terminal power supply, which is usually +5 V, +3.3 V, and voltages close to one volt for the ULSI integrated circuits. The last level, which delivers the power as close as possible (load point), is a Non-Isolated (NI) voltage-lowering converter, called Point-Of-Source regulator (POS), which as a whole is referred to as a POL (Point-Of-Load) or a POU (Point-Of-Use) converter.

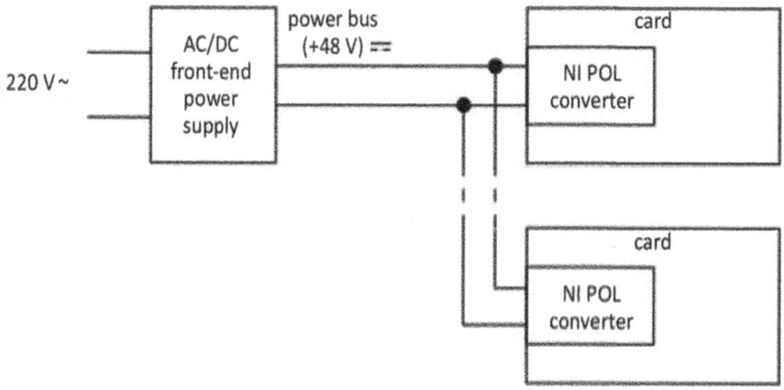

Figure 4.39. *Classical architecture of the power supply by medium voltage for the backplane bus*

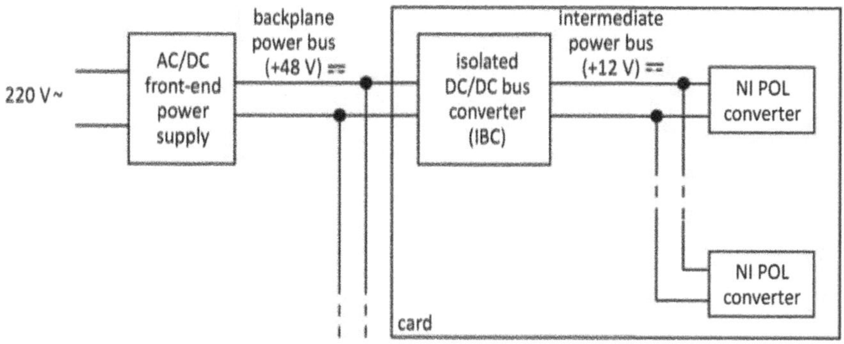

Figure 4.40. *Architecture with intermediate power bus*

Working on the layout of the aforementioned architecture, the modern approach is to insert an intermediate power bus onto the electronic card in order to reduce the amount of energy dissipated during regulation (Figure 4.40). The associated regulator is called an IBC (Isolated Buck Converter)[4]. It isolates the intermediate bus from the backplane bus. The architecture is known as an "Intermediate Bus Architecture"

---

4 This is called BCM® (Bus Converter Module) in the proprietary version by the company Vicor. Some of these modules accept the sector in the input.

(IBA). The low intermediate voltage is usually of +12 V. The aforementioned non-isolated terminal regulators (POL converters) are connected to this power bus. These regulators have a high yield thanks to their – and the bus's – limited voltage swing, and through optimization of the components for a given value of the output voltage and current.

There is a more advanced power supply architecture, called FPA for "Factorized Power Architecture". The approach involves separating the three classical functions of a power supply by localizing them preferentially in a specific area of the system, so as to gain some form of technical advantage. The low value intermediate voltage (7–15 V) is increased (36–55 V) in order to limit the bus current. In this way, it can reduce the surface of the copper by 2/3 compared to the IBA. FPA provides the same functions as IBA, but does so in a different order. The example from Figure 4.41 shows the dual power supply of a microprocessor. A voltage pre-regulator module (PRM) supplies a regulated factorized bus voltage V_F, which is brought to the value of the output voltage by a final regulator called the VTM (Voltage Transformation Module). A VTM is a fixed-ratio current multiplier that transforms the voltage and isolates the input from the output. Its energy yield is in the order of 96%. It should be noted that PRMs like the VTM can be set up in parallel in order to provide more power.

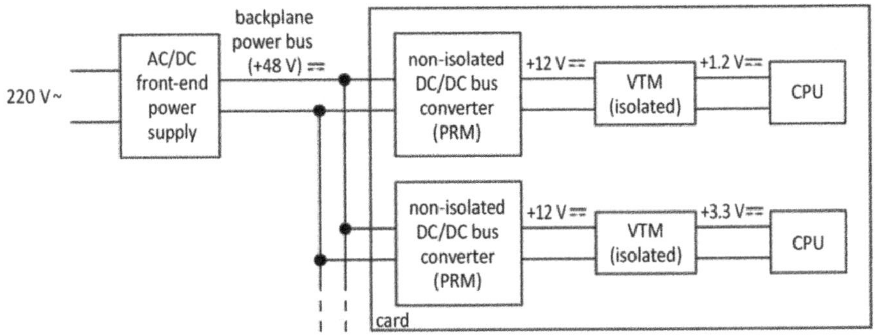

Figure 4.41. *Factorized power supply architecture*

All of these converters can be autonomous, or more or less programmable and monitored. If they are monitored, the information (command/status) passes through a management bus, which is usually a serial bus, as the required bitrate is low. Lastly, depending on the domain in which it is used (portable systems, for example), the energy constraints must be accounted for.

4.3. Summary: bus classifications

Based on the previous categories, another form of classification is possible, one that is different from the classification based on hierarchy from § 4.2, which was categorical. This is shown in Figure 4.42, minus the power bus. It is based on the localization and type of the entity involved. A distinction must be made between the buses that are internal to the component and those that are external to it. For the latter, another distinction must be made, this time between the different levels, which are component or local, board or backplane, system, device or interface, and network. A rule emerges from this classification: the higher the level, the greater the maximal length (Borrill 1981).

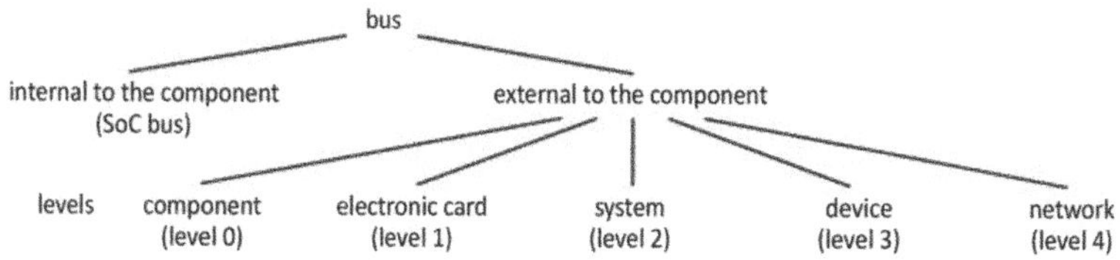

Figure 4.42. *Classification of communication buses*

Bus	Level	Reach	Dependency	Examples of industrial buses
Local	Component	PCB	Processor	Microbus (NS) Z-bus (Zilog)
Backplane	Electronic card	Several cards	None	S-100 Multibus VME STD-bus
System	Rack	Several systems	None	Unibus™ (DEC) Eurobus (Ferranti) BXPbus (Intel)
Device	Electronic card and higher levels	Cards, systems and networks	None	SCSI, USB, IEEE1394
Network	Electronic card and higher levels	Cards, systems and networks	None	CAN, Modbus, Profibus

Table 4.6. *Features of the different bus families*

Table 4.6 contains the main features of each of the external categories.

Conclusion of Volume 2

The bus is a simple and effective shared communication medium that is used for systems with a small number (i.e. a dozen) of nodes. The way it operates is usually fairly simple to understand, and applying it practically tends to be easy for typical operating frequencies. However, it represents a bottleneck in the von Neumann machine model. The memory and the I/O also become bottlenecks if several masters share the same bus. The buses therefore have a key role in computer performances. They have mechanical, electrical, temporal and spatial characteristics, which can be specified in a reference standard, enabling standardization of the electronic and mechanical components, and thus lowering costs. Tests are a topic that has not been covered here, but these are limited due to the heterogeneity of the nodes. The three main topologies are the multipoint and the one-directional (multidrop) bus, as well as the point-to-point link. One way around the heterogeneity of the communicating elements and their data rates, as well as the locality of transfers, is bus hierarchy. The current trend is a shift toward serial buses, using packet-based communication, thus moving away from cycle-based communication. With the advance of integration, buses are disappearing from the motherboard of micro-computers, and instead are to be found on chips, such as the SoC (System-on-Chip). Three works (Del Corso *et al.* 1986; Di Giacomo 1990; Buchanan 2000) further complete the notions covered in this chapter on external buses.

Volume 3 will look at logical sequences, which correspond to the material side of the microprocessor.

Exercises

Below are some exercises that follow on from the notions covered in this work. The number scheme reflects the chapter with which they are associated.

Chapter 1. Exercises

E1.1. Create a logic diagram of a validation system of binary data (format n = 2 bits) using three-state data encoding (*cf.* § 1.4).

Answer. The system has to send an acknowledgment signal when the data is valid, with input values (0, 0) and (1, 1) respectively marking an invalid piece of data, and a non-utilized state. This data can be the result of an operation, in which case the acknowledgment signal is a computation termination signal. Figure E1.53 shows a logic diagram based on a Muller C-element (Muller and Bartky 1959; Muller 1963), the function of which was explained in § 3.4.2 in Darche (2002).

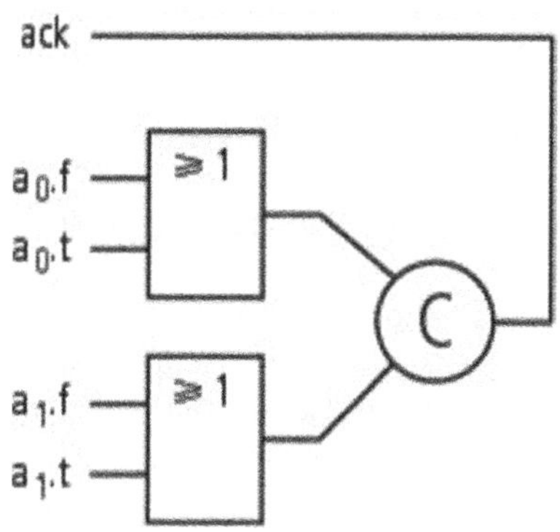

Figure E1.53. *Dual-rail code validation system (n = 2 bits)*

E1.2. What is bus arbitration?

Answer. Arbitration is the mechanism that determines who will be in possession of the bus when there are several simultaneous access requests.

E1.3. Provide two arbiter logic diagrams.

Answer. The two base models are the ripple arbiter and the look-ahead arbiter, whose logic diagrams are shown in Figure E1.54(a) and E1.54(b) respectively. The terms used are similar to those for the natural binary adders (NB(C) for Natural Binary (Code), *cf.* § 2.6.1 in Darche (2002)) in relation to the propagation of internal carries.

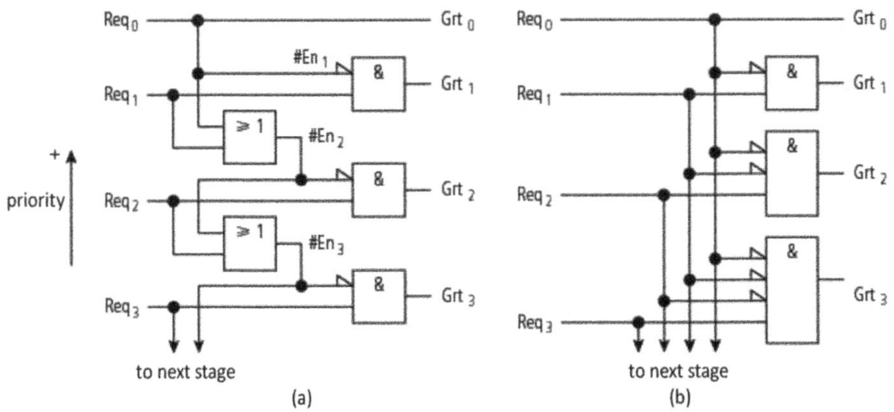

Figure E1.54. *Arbiters with the propagation of serial and look-ahead decisions*

E1.4. With a limit of n = 3 requests, redraw the look-ahead arbitration in order to obtain a daisy chain solution.

Answer. Figure E1.55 shows the logic diagram of the solution.

E1.5. Technological question: what are the criteria for choosing a bus?

Answer. The key criteria are the bitrate and the connection cost. Obviously, there are other parameters too, like the width of the bus, the communication type (synchronous or asynchronous), the protocol, arbitration, etc.

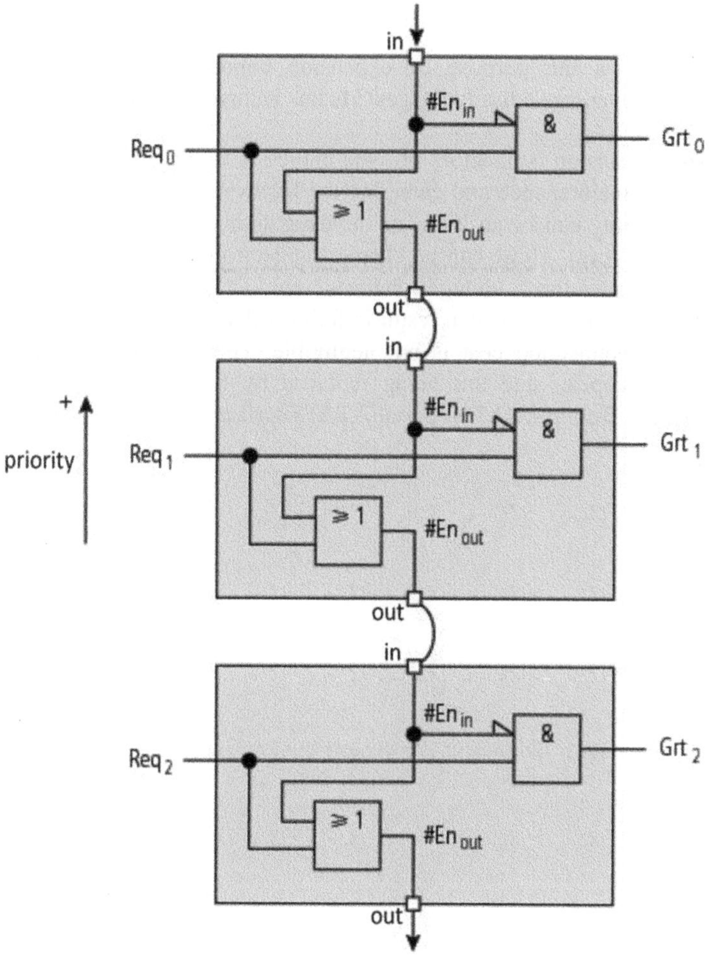

Figure E1.55. *Daisy chain arbiter*

E1.6. How can the performance of a bus be improved?

Answer. Depending on the case, the performance of a bus can be improved by either widening the bus, increasing the serial links or increasing the nominal frequency if it is synchronous (principle of overclocking, which carries its own intrinsic limitations. Particular care has to be made to respecting the maximal heat dissipation of the components). Increasing the valency (i.e. the number of possible significant states of the signal) should not be considered (solution for a network).

Chapter 4. Exercises

E4.1. What is the purpose of expansion connectors in a micro-computer motherboard (advantages/disadvantages)? Is this technically viable in the long-term?

Answer. Expansion connectors provide choice in terms of the material settings, and they make maintenance and changing the hardware easier. However, this has a cost, and reliability can be an issue, as the daughterboard undergoes environmental stresses (of all types). These can be chemical, ElectroStatic Discharge (ESD), dust, changes in temperature, voltage changes, etc. (PVTL for "Process–Voltage–Temperature–Loading"), and can result in failures (bad contacts due to rust or dust). Moreover, the connection cost is not negligible. These expansion connectors are destined to disappear, and are being replaced by high bitrate serial buses, for example the bus from the SATA (Serial ATA) interface.

Acronyms

This section includes all of the acronyms used in this volume. They will be introduced once per chapter.

General

A

A	Address
AB	Alternating-Bit
ABC	Arbitration Bus Controller
AC	Alternating Current
Ack	Acknowledgment
AD	Address/Data
ADC	Analog-to-Digital Converter
AGP	Accelerated Graphics Port
AHB	Advanced High-performance Bus (AMBA)
ALE	Address Latch Enable
AMBA	Arm® Microcontroller Bus Architecture
ARQ	Automatic Repeat request

AS	Address Space
AS	Address Strobe
ASB	Advanced System Bus (AMBA)
AT	Advanced Technology
ATA	AT Attachment
ATAPI	AT Attachment Packet Interface (*cf.* PATA)
ATB	Address Transfer Bus

B

b	bit (*cf.* BIT)
B	Byte
BBusy	Bus Busy
BCM®	Bus Converter Module (by Vicor)
BCT	BiCMOS Technology
BE	Big Endian
BG	Bus Grant
BIOS	Basic Input/Output System
BIT	BInary digiT or Binary digIT
BLVDS	Bus LVDS
BM	Bus Mastering
BPRI	Bus PRiority In
BPRN	Bus PRiority iN
BPRO	Bus PRiority Out
BReq	Bus Request
BSB	Back-Side Bus
BTL	Backplane Transceiver Logic

C

C	Output Clock (*cf.* Clk)
C	Cycle
CAD	Command, Address, Data
CAN	Controller Area Network
CAS	Column Address Strobe (*cf.* CE)
CBTL	CMOS BTL
CBusy	Common Busy
CD	Clock Domain
CD	Collision Detection
CDC	CD Crossing
CE	Chip Enable (*cf.* CS)
CE	Column Enable (abbreviation from JEDEC–JESD88C)
Clk	Clock (*cf.* E)
CMOS	Complementary MOS
Comp	Completion
COTS	Commercial Off-The-Shelf
CPA	Centralized Power (supply) Architecture
CPU	Central Processing Unit
CRC	Cyclic Redundancy Check
CRIMM	Continuity RIMM
CS	Chip Select (*cf.* CE)
CSI	Common System Interface (Intel)
CSMA/CD	Carrier Sense Multiple Access with Collision Detection
CTL	ConTroL

D

D	Data (input)
D	Driver
D-Sub	D-Subminiature (connector)
DC	Direct Current
DDR	Double Data Rate
DE	Driver Enable
DIB	Dual Independent Bus
DMA	Direct Memory Access
DMAC	DMA Controller
DMI	Direct Media Interface (Intel)
DP	Dynamic Priority
DPA	Distributed Power Architecture
DPDRAM	Double Port DRAM
DPS	Distributed Power System
DQ	Data input/output
DQM	DQ Mask
DR	Dual-Rail
DRAM	Dynamic RAM
DTAck	Data Transfer Acknowledge (MC68000)
DTB	Data Transfer Bus

E

E	Clock signal (*cf.* Clk)
E	(Chip) Enable
ECC	Error Checking and Correcting/Error-Correcting Code
ECL	Emitter Coupled Logic
EDC	Error-Detecting Circuit/Code

EISA	Extended ISA
EMC	ElectroMagnetic Compatibility
EMI	ElectroMagnetic Interference
ESD	ElectroStatic Discharge

F

FAST	Fairchild Advanced Schottky TTL
FB+	Futurebus+
FCFS	First-Come First-Served
FDM	Frequency-Division Multiplexing
FIFO	First In, First Out (resource handling)
FPA	Factorized Power (supply) Architecture
FPGA	Field-Programmable Gate Array
FR4	Flame Retardant 4
FSB	Front-Side Bus
FSM	Finite-State Machine
FW	FirmWare

G

G	Ouput Enable (*cf.* OE)
GMCH	Graphics and Memory Controller Hub
Grt	Grant
GTL	Gunning Transceiver Logic
GTLP	GTL Plus

H

H or h	High
HBB	Hierarchical Bus Bridge (architecture)

HD	Hard Disk
HDD	HD Drive
HDL	Hardware Description Language (*cf.* VHDL)
HSBI	High-Speed Backplane Initiative
HT	HyperTransport

I

I	Initiator
iAPX	Intel Advanced Performance Architecture
IBA	Intermediate Bus Architecture
IBC	Isolated Buck Converter
IC	Integrated Circuit
ICH	I/O Controller Hub
ID	IDentification
IDE	Integrated Drive Electronics
IEN	Internet Engineering Note
I/F	InterFace
iLBX™	Local Bus Extension (Intel)
I/O	Input/Output
IO	Input/Output (rarely used)
IOR	I/O Read
IOW	I/O Write
iPSB™	Parallel System Bus (Intel)
IRQ	Interrupt Request
ISA	Instruction Set Architecture
ISA	Industry Standard Architecture
ISBN	International Standard Book Number
iSBX™	Single Board Bus (Intel)

ISP	Integrated System Peripheral (Intel)
iSSB™	Serial System Bus (Intel)

J

JTAG	Joint Test Action Group

L

L or l	Low
LAN	Local Area Network
LDS	Lower Data Strobe
LDT	Lightning Data Transport (AMD) renamed HyperTransport
LE	Little Endian
LSb	Least Significant bit
LSI	Large-Scale Integration
LVD	Low-Voltage Differential
LVDM	LVD Multipoint (TI)
LVDS	LVD Signaling

M

M	Master
M	Memory
MCA	Micro Channel™ Architecture
MCH	Memory Controller Hub
MEMR	MEMory Read
MEMW	MEMory Write
M-LVDS	Multipoint-LVDS
MOS	Metal-Oxide Semiconductor

MPSoC	MultiProcessor SoC
MPU	MicroProcessor Unit
MR	Multi-Rail
MSb	Most Significant bit
MUX	MUltipleXer

N

NAck	Negative Acknowledge
NB(C)	Natural Binary (Code)
NI	Non-isolated
NK	Negative acKnowledgment
NoC	Network-on-Chip
NRZ	Non-Return to Zero

O

OCC	On-Chip Communication
OCC	On-Chip Connection
OE	Output Enable (*cf.* G)
OoO	Out-of-Order
OS	Operating System
OWC	One-Way Command

P

P	Processor
PATA	Parallel ATA
PC	Personal Computer
PCB	Printed Circuit Board
PCI	Peripheral Component Interconnect (standard)

PCI-E or PCIe®	PCI Express
PDE	Power Distribution Element
PDN	Pull-Down Network
PDP	Programmable Data Processor (DEC)
PE	Processing Element, Processor Element
PLC	Programmable Logic Controller
PMOS	Positive (channel) MOS
POL	Point-Of-Load (regulator) (*cf.* POU)
POS	Point-Of-Source (regulator)
POU	Point-Of-Use (converter) (*cf.* POL)
POU	Point-Of-Use (regulator) (*cf.* POL)
PPU	Power Processing Unit
PRM	Pre-Regulator Module
PS/2	Personal System/2 (IBM)
PU	Processing Unit
PUN	Pull-Up Network
PVTL	Process–Voltage–Temperature–Loading

Q

QDR	Quad Data Rate
QPI	Quick Path Interconnect

R

R	Read
R	Repeater
R	Receiver
RAM	Random Access Memory
RAS	Row Address Strobe (*cf.* RE)

Rd	Read
RE	Read Enable
RE	Receiver Enable
RE	Router Element (*cf.* RU)
RE	Row Enable (abbreviation from JEDEC – JESD88C)
REJ	REJect (technique)
Req	Request
RFC	Request For Comments
RFI	Radio-Frequency Interference
RIMM™	Rambus In-line Memory Module
RISC	Reduced Instruction Set Computer
RMW	Read–Modify–Write
ROM	Read-Only Memory
RR	Round Robin
RS	Read Signal
RS	Recommended Standard
RSL	Rambus Signaling Level
RTC	Real-Time Clock
R(T)Z	Return-(To)-Zero
RU	Router Unit (*cf.* RE)
RW or R/W	Read/Write
Rx	Receiver

S

S	Schottky
S	Signal
S	Slave
S	Source

SAck	Selection Acknowledge
SATA	Serial ATA
SCSI	Small Computer System Interface
SDRAM	Synchronous DRAM
SE	Single-Ended
SerDes	Serializer/deserializer
SLI	Scalable Link Interface (Nvidia)
S/N	Signal/Noise (*cf.* SNR)
SNR	Signal-to-Noise Ratio (S/N)
SoC	System on (a) Chip
SONET	Synchronous Optical NETwork
SP	Static Priority
SPD	Serial Presence Detect
SPMT™	Serial Port Memory Technology
SRAM	Static RAM
SREJ	Selective REJect (technique)
SSB	Single Shared Bus (architecture)
SSRAM	Synchronous SRAM
SSTL	Stub Series Terminated Logic
STBus®	Split Transaction Bus

T

T	Target
TDMA	Time-Division Multiple-Access
TLB	Translation Lookaside Buffer
transceiver	transmitter/receiver
TTL	Transistor–Transistor Logic
Tx	Transmitter

U

UDMA	Ultra DMA
UDS	Upper Data Strobe
UI	Unit Interval
ULSI	Ultra LSI
USB	Universal Serial Bus

V

VAN	Vehicle Area Network
VHDL	VHSIC Hardware Description Language
VHSIC	Very High-Speed Integrated Circuit
VL-Bus or VLB	VESA Local Bus or Video Local Bus
VLSI	Very LSI
VM	Virtual Memory
VME	Versa Module European
VTM	Voltage Transformation Module

W

W	Wait
W	Wrapper
W	Write
WE	Write Enable
Wr	Write (signal)
WS	Write Signal

X

XT	eXtended Technology (IBM)

Others

μC	Microcomputer
μP	Microprocessor
2D or 2-D	Two-dimensional
4D or 4-D	Four-dimensional

Measurement units or unit prefixes

b/s or bps	bit per second
B/s or Bps	byte per second
G	giga (= 10^9)
Gb	gigabit
Gb/s or Gbps	gigabit per second
GB	gigabyte
GB/s or GBps	gigabyte per second
k	kilo (= 1000)
kb	kilobit (= 1000 b)
kb/s or kbps	kilobit per second
kB	kilobyte (1000 bytes)
kB/s or kBps	kilobyte per second
Kibi	kilobinary (prefix Ki = 2^{10})
KiB	kibibyte (= 2^{10} bytes)
M	mega (= 10^6)
Mb	megabit
Mb/s or Mbps	megabit per second
MB	megabyte
MB/s or MBps	megabyte per second
T	tera (= 10^{12})
Tb	terabit

Tb/s or Tbps	terabit per second
TB	terabyte
TB/s or TBps	terabyte per second

Voltage features

Gnd	Ground
V_{CC}	Collector DC supply voltage
V_d	Direct voltage
V_{DD}	Drain DC supply voltage
V_{DDQ}	Output stage drain power voltage (JEDEC)
V_{ref}	Reference voltage
V_{SS}	Source–Source voltage
V_T	Threshold voltage
V_{TT}	TerminaTion rail voltage

Temporal characteristics

t_a	access time
t_{acc} or t_{ACC}	access time
t_{AH}	Address Hold time
t_{AV}	Address Valid time to E (rise)
t_c or t_{cyc}	cycle time
t_{DDW}	Write Data Delay time
t_{DHR}	Read Data Hold time
t_{DHW}	Write Data Hold time
t_{dis}	disable time (of a three-state output)
t_{DSR}	Read Data Setup time
t_{flight}	flight time
t_h or t_{hold}	hold time

t_{pd} or t_{po}	propagation delay time
t_{su} or t_{setup}	setup time

Company or body

ACM	Association for Computing Machinery
AFIPS	American Federation of Information Processing Societies
AFISI	Association Française d'Ingénierie des Systèmes d'Information
AMD	Advanced Micro Devices, Inc.
ANSI	American National Standards Institute
ARM	Acorn RISC Machine, later Advanced RISC Machines
DEC	Digital Equipment Corporation
DIN	Deutsches Institut für Normung
EIA	Electronic Industries Association, later Electronic Industries Alliance
HP	Hewlett-Packard
IBM	International Business Machines Corporation
IDT	Integrated Device Technology
IEC	International Electrotechnical Commission
IEEE	Institute of Electrical and Electronics Engineers
ISO	International Organization for Standardization, Organisation Internationale de Standardisation
ISSCC	IEEE International Solid-State Circuits Conference
JEDEC	Joint Electron Device Engineering Council (Solid-State Technology Association)
MIT	Massachussets Institute of Technology
MITS	Micro Instrumentation Telemetry Systems
MPR	Microprocessor Report
NS	National Semiconductor
OIF	Optical Internetworking Forum

OSI	Open Systems Interconnection
PCI-SIG	PCI Special Interest Group
PSA	Peugeot Société Anonyme
SGI	Silicon Graphics, Inc.
TI	Texas Instruments
TIA	Telecommunications Industry Association
VESA	Video Electronics Standards Association
VITA	VMEbus International Trade Association

Trademarks - ™

Gigaplane	Sun
iLBX	Intel
iPSB	Intel
iSBX	Intel
iSSB	Intel
i486	Intel Corporation
MCA	Micro Channel
Micro Channel	IBM (*cf.* MCA)
Pentium	Intel Corporation
PowerPath-2	SGI
RIMM	Rambus (*cf.* CRIMM)
SPMT	Consortium SPMT, LLC
VMEbus	Motorola Incorporated

Registered trademark – ®

AMD	AMD
Arm	Arm Limited
BCM	Vicor

DEC	Digital Equipment Corporation
DIGITAL	Digital Equipment Corporation
Fairchild	Fairchild Semiconductor Corporation
Intel	Intel
Micro Channel	IBM Corporation
Multibus	Intel Corporation
OMNIBUS	Digital Equipment Corporation
PCIe	PCI-SIG
PDP	Digital Equipment Corporation
Pentium	Intel
PS/2	International Business Machines Corporation
Rambus	Rambus Inc.
RapidIO	RapidIO.org
STBus	STMicroelectronics
TRI-STATE	NS

References

Preface

Darche, P. (2000). *Architecture des ordinateurs – Représentation des nombres et codes – Cours avec exercices corrigés*. Éditions Gaëtan Morin. November.

Darche, P. (2002). *Architecture des ordinateurs – Fonctions booléennes, logiques combinatoire et séquentielle – Cours avec exercices et exemples en VHDL*. Éditions Vuibert. March.

Darche P. (2003). *Architecture des ordinateurs - Interfaces et périphériques - Cours avec exercices corrigés*. Editions Vuibert. June.

Darche, P. (2004). *Architecture des ordinateurs - Logique booléenne: implémentations et technologies*. Editions Vuibert. November.

Darche, P. (2012). *Mémoires à semi-conducteurs: principe de fonctionnement et organisation interne des mémoires vives - Volume 1*. Editions Vuibert. January. Un des quatre ouvrages sélectionnés pour le prix AFISI (Association Française d'Ingénierie des Systèmes d'Information) du meilleur livre informatique.

Chapters 1 to 4

ANSI/IEEE (1982a). IEEE Standard Microcomputer System Bus. ANSI/IEEE Std 796–1983. Approved December 9, 1982 by IEEE Standards Board, Approved February 17, 1984 by American National Standards Institute.

ANSI/IEEE (1982b). IEEE Standard 696 Interface Devices. IEEE Std 696–1983. Approved June 10, by IEEE Standards Board, Approved September 8, 1983 by American National Standards Institute.

ANSI/TIA/EIA (2002). Electrical Characteristics of Multipoint-Low-Voltage Differential Signaling (M-LVDS) Interface Circuits for Multipoint Data Interchange. TIA/EIA Standard ANSI/TIA/EIA-899-2002. Approved February 26.

Bell, C.G., Kotok, A., Hastings, T.N., and Hill, R. (1978). The Evolution of the DECsystem 10. *Communications of the ACM (CACM)*, 21(1), 44–63. January.

van Berkel, K. and Bink, A. (1996). Single-track handshake signaling with application to micropipelines and handshake circuits. *Second International Symposium on Advanced Research in Asynchronous Circuits and Systems*, 122–133. March 18–21, Aizu-Wakamatsu, Fukushima, Japan.

Borrill, P.L. (1981). The microprocessor bus structures and standards. *IEEE Micro*, 1(1), 84–95. February.

Borrill, P.L. (1988). Limits of backplane bus design. 1988 IEEE International Conference on Computer Design: VLSI in Computers and Processors (ICCD'88), 236–239. October 3–5.

Borrill, P. and Theus, J. (1984). An advanced communication protocol for the proposed IEEE 896 Futurebus. *IEEE Micro*, 4(4), 42–56. August.

Buchanan, W. (2000). *Computer Busses.* Arnold.

Budruk, R., Anderson, D. and Shanley, T. (2003). In *PCI Express System Architecture*, Winkles, J. (ed.). PC System Architecture Series. Addison-Wesley Developer's Press. MindShare, Inc.

Carey, B.J. and Grossman, H. (1977). Assembling a complex breadboard can be as easy as 1,2,3. *Electronics*, 50(20), 104–109. Republished in (Lyman 1980).

Chen, J.Y., Jone, W.B., Wang, J.S., Lu, H.-I., and Chen, T.F. (1999). Segmented bus design for low-power systems. *IEEE Transactions on Very Large Scale Integration (VLSI) Systems*, 7(1), 25–29. April.

Childers, B.A. and Baden, E.A. (1997). Bus bridge address translator. American patent no. 5634013. Application number: 08/434183. Filing date: May 3, 1995. Publication date: May 27.

Cohen, D. (1981). On holy wars and a plea for peace. *IEEE Computer*, 14(10), 48–54. October 1981. Original: IEN (Internet Engineering Note) 137. USC/ISI (University of Southern California /Information Sciences Institute). April 1.

Colmenar, J.M., Garnica, O., Lanchares, J., and Hidalgo, J.I. (2009). Characterizing asynchronous variable latencies through probability distribution functions. *Microprocessors and Microsystems*, 33(7–8), 483–497. October-November.

Corral, J.M.R., Balcells, A.C., Moreno, G.J., Estévez, A.M., and Barranco, A.L. (2002). Application of bus emulation techniques to the design of a PCI/MC68000 bridge. *Microprocessors and Microsystems*, 26(8), 373–389. November 10.

Corso, D.D., Kirrmann, H., and Nicoud, J.-D. (1986). *Microcomputer Buses and Links.* Academic Press Inc.

Cowan, A.S. and Whitehead, D.G. (1976). Asynchronous polling arbiter. *Electronics Letters*, 12(2), 43–44. November 24.

Crisp, R., Donnelly, K., Moncayo, A., Perino, D., and Zerbe, J. (1997). Development of single-chip multi-GB/s DRAMs. *44th IEEE International Solid-State Circuits Conference (ISSCC 1997)*, 226–227 and 461. February 6–8.

Dally, W.J. and Towles, B. (2001). Route packets, not wires: On-chip inteconnection networks. *38th Annual Design Automation Conference (DAC'01)*, 684–689. June 18–22. Las Vegas, NV, USA.

Dandamudi, S. (2003). Fundamentals of Computer Organization and Design. Springer.

Darche, P. (2000). *Architecture des ordinateurs – Représentation des nombres et codes – Cours avec exercices corrigés*. Éditions Gaëtan Morin, November.

Darche, P. (2002). *Architecture des ordinateurs – Fonctions booléennes, logiques combinatoire et séquentielle – Cours avec exercices et exemples en VHDL*. Éditions Vuibert, March.

Darche, P. (2003). *Architecture des ordinateurs - Interfaces et périphériques - Cours avec exercices corrigés*. Editions Vuibert, June.

Darche, P. (2004). *Architecture des ordinateurs - Logique booléenne: implémentations et technologies*. Editions Vuibert, November.

Darche, P. (2012). *Mémoires à semi-conducteurs: principe de fonctionnement et organisation interne des mémoires vives - Volume 1*. Editions Vuibert, 556, January. Un des quatre ouvrages sélectionnés pour le prix AFISI (Association Française d'Ingénierie des Systèmes d'Information) du meilleur livre informatique.

DeBock, R. (1982). VERSAbus – a multiprocessor bus standard – and VMEbus – its Eurocard counterpart. *Microprocessors and Microsystems*, 6(9), 475–481, November.

DEC (1970). PDP-8/E, PDP-8/M & PDP-8/F Small Computer Handbook. PDP-8 Handbook Series. Digital Equipment Corporation.

DeFalco, J.A. (1970). Reflection and crosstalk in logic circuit interconnections. *IEEE Spectrum*, 7(7), 44–50. July.

EIA (1991). Interface Between Data Terminal Equipment and Data Circuit-Terminating Equipment Employing Serial Binary Data Interchange. Standard ANSI/EIA/TIA-232-E. Electronic Industries Association (EIA). July.

EIA (1997). Interface Between Data Terminal Equipment and Data Circuit-Terminating Equipment Employing Serial Binary Data Interchange. Standard ANSI/EIA/TIA-232-F. Electronic Industries Association (EIA). October.

Fairhurst, G. and Wood, L. (2002). Advice to link designers on link automatic repeat request (ARQ). Request for comments (RFC) 3366. August.

Feldman, M., Vaidyanathan, R., and El-Amawy, A. (1999). High speed, high capacity bused interconnects using optical slab waveguides. *11th IPPS/SPDP'99 Workshop*, held in conjunction with the *13th International Parallel Processing Symposium* and *10th Symposium on Parallel and Distributed Processing (IPPS/SPDP'99)*. Lecture Notes in Computer Science (LNCS), vol. 1586, 924–937. April 12–16, San Juan (Porto Rico), USA.

Finkelstein, E. and Weiss, S. (1999). Microprocessor system buses: A case study. *Journal of Systems Architecture*, 45(1213), 1151–1168. June.

Furber, S.B. and Day, P. (1996). Four-phase micropipeline latch control circuits. *IEEE Transactions on Very Large Scale Integration (VLSI)*, 4(2), 247–253. June.

Furber, S.B. and Liu, J. (1996). Dynamic logic in four-phase micropipelines. *Second International Symposium on Advanced Research in Asynchronous Circuits and Systems*, 11–16. March 18–21.

Galles, M. and Williams, E. (1994). Performance optimizations, implementation, and verification of the SGI challenge multiprocessor. *Twenty-Seventh Hawaii International Conference on System Sciences*, 1, 134–143. 4–7 January.

Gebali, F., Elmiligi, H., and El-Kharashi, M.W. (2009). *Networks on Chips - Theory and Practice.* Gebali, F., Elmiligi, H., and El-Kharashi, M.W. (eds). CRC Press.

Giacomo, J.D. (1990). *Digital Bus Handbook.* Mc Graw-Hill Book Company, Inc.

Gray, J. and Shenay, P. (1999). Rules of thumb in data engineering. December 1. *16th International Conference on Data Engineering (ICDE'00)*, 3. February 28 – March 03, 2000.

Guibaly, F.E. (1989). Design and analysis of arbitration protocols. *IEEE Transactions on Computers*, 38 (2), 161–171. February.

Gunning, W.F. (1991). Drivers and receivers for interfacing VLSI CMOS circuits to transmission lines. United States patent 5023488. Application date: 07/502372. Publication date: June 11. Filing date: March 30, 1990.

Gustavson, D.B. and Theus, J. (1983). Wire-OR logic on transmission lines. *IEEE Micro*, 3(3), 51–55. June.

Holden, B., Trodden, J., and Anderson, D. (2008). *HyperTransport 3.1 Interconnect Technology*. MindShare, Inc.. MindShare Press.

IEEE (1984). P959 I/O Expansion bus proposed standard. *IEEE Micro*, 4(3), 33–54. June.

IEEE (1985). IEEE Standards for Local Area Networks: Carrier Sense Multiple Access with Collision Detection (CSMA/CD) Access Method and Physical Layer Specifications. ANSI/IEEE Std 802.3-1985. The Institute of Electrical and Electronics Engineers. New York.

IEEE (1987). IEEE Standard for A Versatile Backplane Bus: VMEbus. ANSI/IEEE IEEE Std 1014™-1987(R2008). Approved 12 March 1987 by IEEE Standards Board, Approved 11 September 1987 by American National Standards Institute.

IEEE (1988). IEEE Standard for a High-Performance Synchronous 32-Bit Bus: MULTIBUS II. ANSI/IEEE Std 1296-1987. Approved June 11, 1987 by IEEE Standards Board, Approved February 8, 1988 by American National Standards Institute.

IEEE (1989). IEEE Standard FASTBUS Modular High-Speed Data Acquisition and Control System and IEEE FASTBUS Standard Routines. ANSI/IEEE Std 960-1989. Approved October 11, 1989 by IEEE Standards Board. Approved February 26, 1990 by American National Standards Institute.

IEEE (1991). IEEE Standard for Futurebus+ – Logical Protocol Specification. IEEE Std 896.1-1991 (Revision of IEEE Std 896.1-1987). Approved September 26.

IEEE (1994). Information Technology - Microprocessor Systems – Futurebus+ – Logical Protocol Specification. ISO/IEC Standard 10857. ANSI/IEEE Std 896.1. First edition. April 27.

IEEE (2002a). Draft Standard for Prefixes for Binary Multiples. IEEE Std P1541/D5. The Institute of Electrical and Electronics Engineers. New York, USA. April 18.

IEEE (2002b). IEEE Std 1541-2002: IEEE Standard for Prefixes for Binary Multiples.

IEEE (2008). IEEE Standard for Information Technology – Telecommunications and Information Exchange between Systems – Local and Metropolitan Area Networks – Specific Requirements. Part 3: Carrier Sense Multiple Access with Collision Detection (CSMA/CD) Access Method and Physical Layer Specifications. IEEE Std 802.3™-2008 (Revision of IEEE Std 802.3-2005). The Institute of Electrical and Electronics Engineers. New York, USA. December 26.

IEEE (2013). Standard for Test Access Port and Boundary-Scan Architecture. IEEE Std 1149.1 -2013 (Revision of IEEE Std 1149.1-2001). Approved February 6.

Intel (1989). Intel ISA Bus Specification and Application Notes. Rev. 2.01. Intel Corporation. September 12.

Intel (1997). Pentium® II Processor GTL+ Guidelines. Application Note AP-585. Intel. May. Order Number: 243330-001.

Jackson, M. and Budruk, R. (2012). PCI Express Technology. Comprehensive Guide to Generations 1.x, 2.x and 3.0. MindShare Technology Series. MindShare, Inc.

James, D.V. (1990). Multiplexed buses: The endian wars continue. *IEEE Micro*, 10(3), 9–21. May/June.

JEDEC (2007). Gunning Transceiver Logic (GTL) Low-Level, High-Speed Interface Standard for Digital Integrated Circuits. JEDEC Standard JESD8-3A (Revision of JESD8-3, November 1993). Addendum no. 3A to JESD8. May.

Kipnis, S. (1989). Priority arbitration with busses. technical report MIT/LCS/TM-408. Laboratory for Computer Science, Massachusetts Institute of Technology (MIT). October.

Kushiyama, N., Ohshima, S., Stark, D.C., Sakurai, K., Takase, S., Furuyuma, T., Barth, R.M., Dillon, J., Gasbarro, J.A., Griffin, M.M., Horowitz, M., Lee, V., Lee, W.K.M., and Leung, W. (1992). 500 Mbyte/sec data-rate 512 Kbits × 9 DRAM using a novel I/O interface. *Symposium on VLSI Circuit*, 66–67. June 4–6.

Leiserson, C.E. (1985). Fat trees: Universal networks for hardware-efficient supercomputing. *IEEE Transactions on Computers*, 34(10), 892–901. October.

Lyman, J. (1980). In *Microelectronics: Interconnection and Packaging*, Lyman, J. (ed.). Electronics Book Series. McGraw-Hill.

McCluskey, E.J. (1962). Fundamental mode and pulse mode (operations of) sequential circuits. *1962 International Federation For Information Processing Congress (IFIP 62)*, 725–730. August 27 – September 1, Munich, Germany. North Holland Publishing Company 1963.

Messerschmitt, D.G. (1990). Synchronization in digital system design. *IEEE Journal on Selected Areas in Communications*, 8(8), 1404–1419. October 1990.

Muller, D.E. (1963). Asynchronous logics and application to information processing. In *Switching Theory in Space Technology*. Aiken, H. and Main, W.F. (eds). Stanford University Press.

Muller, D.E. and Bartky, W.S. (1959). *A Theory of Asynchronous Circuits*. The annals of the computation laboratory of Harvard University, 204–243. Harvard University Press. Cambridge, Massachusetts.

Nicoud, J.D. (1987). Principles and comparison of major buses. *Europhysics Conference on Control Systems for Experimental Physics*, 467–490. September 28 – October 2, Villars-sur-Ollon, Switzerland.

Nyström, M. and Martin, A.J. (2002). *Asynchronous Pulse Logic*. Kluwer Academic Publishers.

Okazawa, K., Osaka, H. and Saitou, K. (1998). Increasing Data Transfer Efficiency for a Read Operation in a Non-Split Transaction Bus Environment by Substituting a Write Operation for the Read Operation. American patent no. 5754802. Application number: 08/648424. Filing date: May 15, 1996. Publication date: May 19.

OpenCores (2010). Wishbone B4 WISHBONE System-on-Chip (SoC) Interconnection Architecturefor Portable IP Cores. OpenCores.

Pasricha, S. and Dutt, N. (2008). On-Chip Communication Architectures: System on Chip Interconnect. Morgan Kaufmann Publishers.

PCI-SIG (1993a). PCI Local Bus Specification. Revision 2.0. Intel Corporation. April 30.

PCI-SIG (1993b). PCI System Design Guide. Revision 1.0. Intel Corporation. September 8.

PCI-SIG (1998). PCI Local Bus Specification, Revision 2.2. PCI-SIG (Special Interest Group). December 18.

PCI-SIG (2002). PCI Local Bus Specification. Revision 3.0. PCI-SIG (Special Interest Group). August 12.

Plummer, W.W. (1972). Asynchronous arbiters. *IEEE Transactions on Computers*, C-21(1), 37–42. January.

Renaudin, M. (2000). Asynchronous circuits and systems: A promising design alternative. *Microelectronic Engineering*, 54(1–2), 133–149. December.

Roberts, H.E. and Yates, W. (1975a). ALTAIR 8800: The most powerful minicomputer project ever presented - can be built for under $400. ALTAIR 8800 Minicomputer, Part I. *Popular Electronics*, 7(1), 33–38. January.

Roberts, H.E. and Yates, W. (1975b). Build the ALTAIR minicomputer. ALTAIR 8800 minicomputer, Part II. *Popular Electronics*, 7(2), 56–58. February.

Savage, N. (2002). Linking with light. *IEEE Spectrum*, 39(8), 32–36. August.

Schmidt, F. (1995). The SCSI Bus and IDE Interface: Protocols, Applications and Programming. Addison-Wesley Publishing Company, Inc.

Shanley, T. and Anderson, D. (1995a). *ISA System Architecture.* MindShare, Inc. Addison-Wesley Developers Press.

Shanley, T. and Anderson, D. (1995b). *EISA System Architecture.* MindShare, Inc. Addison-Wesley Developers Press.

Shanley, T. and Anderson, D. (1995c). *PCI System Architecture.* MindShare, Inc. Addison-Wesley Developers Press.

Shannon, C.E. (1948). A mathematical theory of communication. *The Bell System Technical Journal*, 27, 379. Republished in (Shannon 1993).

Shannon, C.E. (1993). Claude Elwood Shannon, Collected Papers. Sloane, N.J.A. and Wyner, A.D. (eds), IEEE Press.

Slater, M. (1992). Rambus unveils revolutionary memory interface. *Microprocessor Report (MPR)*, 15–21. March 4.

Solari, E. (1994). *ISA & EISA Theory and Operation.* Annabooks 1992, 1993.

Soltero, J.M. and Cox, E. (2002). Logic in live-insertion applications with a focus on GTLP. Application report SCEA026. Texas Instruments. February.

Sriti, M. (1999). System for performing DMA byte swapping within each data element in accordance to swapping indication bits within a DMA command. Application number: 08/616594. Filing date: March 15, 1996. Publication date: January 19.

Stan, M.R. and Burleson, W.P. (1995). Bus-invert coding for low-power I/O. *IEEE Transaction on VLSI Systems*, 3(1), 49–58. March.

Stern, R.H. (2001a). Preventing abuse of IEEE standards policy. Micro law. *IEEE Micro*, 21(3), 8–11. May/June.

Stern, R.H. (2001b). More standardization skullduggery. Micro law. *IEEE Micro*, 21(4), 12–15, 69. July/August.

Stern, R.H. (2001c). Another update on standardization skullduggery. Micro law. *IEEE Micro*, 21(5), 8–10. September/October.

Stern, R.H. (2002). FTC piles onto standardization rambus' skullduggery. Micro law. *IEEE Micro*, 22(4), 6–7, 86–87. July/August.

Stern, R.H. (2003). Weird turn of events in continuing rambus saga. Micro law. *IEEE Micro*, 23(1), 76–80. January/February.

Stern, R.H. (2007). Coming down the home stretch in the rambus standardization skullduggery saga: To levy or not to levy royalties. Micro law. *IEEE Micro*, 27(2), 80–82. March/April.

Stern, R.H. (2009). One of the last updates on rambus standardization skullduggery. Micro law. *IEEE Micro*, 29(1), 139–143. January/February.

Strassberg, D. (1999). Digital buses, analog problems. *EDN*, Design Feature. 73–74, 76–78, 81, 83, 85–86. May 27.

Sutherland, I.E. (1989, 2007). Micropipelines. *Communications of the ACM (CACM)*, 32(6), 720–738. June. Also in *ACM Turing Award Lectures Book*, Year Awarded 1988.

Tabisz, W.A., Jovanovic, M.M., and Lee, F.C. (1992). Present and future of distributed power systems. *7th Annual Conference of Applied Power Electronics Conference (APEC'92)*, 11–18. February 23–27.

Taub, M.D. (1984). Arbitration and control acquisition in the proposed IEEE 896 futurebus. *IEEE Micro*, 4(4), 28–41. August.

Thurber, K.J., Jensen, E.D., Jack, L.A., Kinney, L.L., Patton, P.C., and Anderson, L.C. (1972). A systematic approach to the design of digital bussing structures. *Fall Joint Computer Conference (AFIPS'72)*, Part II, 719–740, December 5–7.

TI (1983). *NuBus Specification* – Nu Machine. Texas Instruments Incorporated.

TIA (2001). Electrical Characteristics of Unbalanced Voltage Digital Interface Circuits. Standard TIA/EIA-423-B. Telecommunications Industry Association. November 20.

Trodden, J. and Anderson, D. (2003). *HyperTransport™ System Architecture*. MindShare, Inc. Addison-Wesley.

Ware, F.A, Barth, R.M., Stark, D.C., Hampel, C.E., Tsern, E.K., Abhyankar, A.M., Holman, T.J., Anderson, A.V., and Macwilliams, P.D. (2001). Apparatus and method for bus timing compensation. American patent no. 6226757. Filing date: October 9, 1998. Publication date: May 1.

Weiss, S. and Finkelstein, E. (1999). Extending PCI performance beyond the desktop. *IEEE Computer*, 32(6), 80–87. June.

Widmer, A.X. and Franaszek, P.A. (1983). A DC-balanced, partitioned-block, 8B/10B transmission code. *IBM Journal of Research and Development*, 27(5), 440–451. September.

Yang, J., Gupta, R., and Zhang, C. (2004). Frequent value encoding for low power data buses. *ACM Transactions on Design Automation of Electronic Systems*, 9(3), 354–384. July.

Zhang, Y., Ye, W., and Irwin, M.J. (1998). An alternative architecture for on-chip global interconnect segmented bus power modeling. *Thirty-Second Asilomar Conference on Signals, Systems and Computers*, 2, 1062–1065. November 1–4, Pacific Grove, CA, USA.

Zilog (1985). Z·BUS® Component Interconnect – Summary. Zilog. April.

Index

This index covers all 5 volumes in this series of books.

B

C

D

E

F

G

H

I

J

L

M

N

O

S

T

U

V

W

Other titles from

ISTE

in

Computer Engineering

2020

LAFFLY Dominique
TORUS 1 – Toward an Open Resource Using Services: Cloud Computing for Environmental Data
TORUS 2 – Toward an Open Resource Using Services: Cloud Computing for Environmental Data
TORUS 3 – Toward an Open Resource Using Services: Cloud Computing for Environmental Data

LAURENT Anne, LAURENT Dominique, MADERA Cédrine
Data Lakes
(Databases and Big Data Set – Volume 2)

OULHADJ Hamouche, DAACHI Boubaker, MENASRI Riad
Metaheuristics for Robotics
(Optimization Heuristics Set – Volume 2)

SADIQUI Ali
Computer Network Security

2019

BESBES Walid, DHOUIB Diala, WASSAN Niaz, MARREKCHI Emna
Solving Transport Problems: Towards Green Logistics

CLERC Maurice
Iterative Optimizers: Difficulty Measures and Benchmarks

GHLALA Riadh
Analytic SQL in SQL Server 2014/2016

TOUNSI Wiem
Cyber-Vigilance and Digital Trust: Cyber Security in the Era of Cloud Computing and IoT

2018

ANDRO Mathieu
Digital Libraries and Crowdsourcing
(Digital Tools and Uses Set – Volume 5)

ARNALDI Bruno, GUITTON Pascal, MOREAU Guillaume
Virtual Reality and Augmented Reality: Myths and Realities

BERTHIER Thierry, TEBOUL Bruno
From Digital Traces to Algorithmic Projections

CARDON Alain
Beyond Artificial Intelligence: From Human Consciousness to Artificial Consciousness

HOMAYOUNI S. Mahdi, FONTES Dalila B.M.M.
Metaheuristics for Maritime Operations
(Optimization Heuristics Set – Volume 1)

JEANSOULIN Robert
JavaScript and Open Data

PIVERT Olivier
NoSQL Data Models: Trends and Challenges
(Databases and Big Data Set – Volume 1)

SEDKAOUI Soraya
Data Analytics and Big Data

SALEH Imad, AMMI Mehdi, SZONIECKY Samuel
Challenges of the Internet of Things: Technology, Use, Ethics
(Digital Tools and Uses Set – Volume 7)

SZONIECKY Samuel
Ecosystems Knowledge: Modeling and Analysis Method for Information and Communication
(Digital Tools and Uses Set – Volume 6)

2017

BENMAMMAR Badr
Concurrent, Real-Time and Distributed Programming in Java

HÉLIODORE Frédéric, NAKIB Amir, ISMAIL Boussaad, OUCHRAA Salma, SCHMITT Laurent
Metaheuristics for Intelligent Electrical Networks
(Metaheuristics Set – Volume 10)

MA Haiping, SIMON Dan
Evolutionary Computation with Biogeography-based Optimization
(Metaheuristics Set – Volume 8)

PÉTROWSKI Alain, BEN-HAMIDA Sana
Evolutionary Algorithms
(Metaheuristics Set – Volume 9)

PAI G A Vijayalakshmi
Metaheuristics for Portfolio Optimization
(Metaheuristics Set – Volume 11)

2016

BLUM Christian, FESTA Paola
Metaheuristics for String Problems in Bio-informatics
(Metaheuristics Set – Volume 6)

DEROUSSI Laurent
Metaheuristics for Logistics
(Metaheuristics Set – Volume 4)

DHAENENS Clarisse and JOURDAN Laetitia
Metaheuristics for Big Data
(Metaheuristics Set – Volume 5)

LABADIE Nacima, PRINS Christian, PRODHON Caroline
Metaheuristics for Vehicle Routing Problems
(Metaheuristics Set – Volume 3)

LEROY Laure
Eyestrain Reduction in Stereoscopy

LUTTON Evelyne, PERROT Nathalie, TONDA Albert
Evolutionary Algorithms for Food Science and Technology
(Metaheuristics Set – Volume 7)

MAGOULÈS Frédéric, ZHAO Hai-Xiang
Data Mining and Machine Learning in Building Energy Analysis

RIGO Michel
Advanced Graph Theory and Combinatorics

2015

BARBIER Franck, RECOUSSINE Jean-Luc
COBOL Software Modernization: From Principles to Implementation with the BLU AGE® Method

CHEN Ken
Performance Evaluation by Simulation and Analysis with Applications to Computer Networks

CLERC Maurice
Guided Randomness in Optimization
(Metaheuristics Set – Volume 1)

DURAND Nicolas, GIANAZZA David, GOTTELAND Jean-Baptiste, ALLIOT Jean-Marc
Metaheuristics for Air Traffic Management
(Metaheuristics Set – Volume 2)

MAGOULÈS Frédéric, ROUX François-Xavier, HOUZEAUX Guillaume
Parallel Scientific Computing

MUNEESAWANG Paisarn, YAMMEN Suchart
Visual Inspection Technology in the Hard Disk Drive Industry

2014

BOULANGER Jean-Louis
Formal Methods Applied to Industrial Complex Systems

BOULANGER Jean-Louis
Formal Methods Applied to Complex Systems:Implementation of the B Method

GARDI Frédéric, BENOIST Thierry, DARLAY Julien, ESTELLON Bertrand, MEGEL Romain
Mathematical Programming Solver based on Local Search

KRICHEN Saoussen, CHAOUACHI Jouhaina
Graph-related Optimization and Decision Support Systems

LARRIEU Nicolas, VARET Antoine
Rapid Prototyping of Software for Avionics Systems: Model-oriented Approaches for Complex Systems Certification

OUSSALAH Mourad Chabane
Software Architecture 1
Software Architecture 2

PASCHOS Vangelis Th
Combinatorial Optimization – 3-volume series, 2nd Edition
Concepts of Combinatorial Optimization – Volume 1, 2nd Edition
Problems and New Approaches – Volume 2, 2nd Edition
Applications of Combinatorial Optimization – Volume 3, 2nd Edition

QUESNEL Flavien
Scheduling of Large-scale Virtualized Infrastructures: Toward Cooperative Management

RIGO Michel
Formal Languages, Automata and Numeration Systems 1: Introduction to Combinatorics on Words
Formal Languages, Automata and Numeration Systems 2: Applications to Recognizability and Decidability

SAINT-DIZIER Patrick
Musical Rhetoric: Foundations and Annotation Schemes

TOUATI Sid, DE DINECHIN Benoit
Advanced Backend Optimization

2013

ANDRÉ Etienne, SOULAT Romain
The Inverse Method: Parametric Verification of Real-time Embedded Systems

BOULANGER Jean-Louis
Safety Management for Software-based Equipment

DELAHAYE Daniel, PUECHMOREL Stéphane
Modeling and Optimization of Air Traffic

FRANCOPOULO Gil
LMF — Lexical Markup Framework

GHÉDIRA Khaled
Constraint Satisfaction Problems

ROCHANGE Christine, UHRIG Sascha, SAINRAT Pascal
Time-Predictable Architectures

WAHBI Mohamed
Algorithms and Ordering Heuristics for Distributed Constraint Satisfaction Problems

ZELM Martin *et al.*
Enterprise Interoperability

2012

ARBOLEDA Hugo, ROYER Jean-Claude
Model-Driven and Software Product Line Engineering

BLANCHET Gérard, DUPOUY Bertrand
Computer Architecture

BOULANGER Jean-Louis
Industrial Use of Formal Methods: Formal Verification

BOULANGER Jean-Louis
Formal Method: Industrial Use from Model to the Code

CALVARY Gaëlle, DELOT Thierry, SÈDES Florence, TIGLI Jean-Yves
Computer Science and Ambient Intelligence

MAHOUT Vincent
Assembly Language Programming: ARM Cortex-M3 2.0: Organization, Innovation and Territory

MARLET Renaud
Program Specialization

SOTO Maria, SEVAUX Marc, ROSSI André, LAURENT Johann
Memory Allocation Problems in Embedded Systems: Optimization Methods

2011

BICHOT Charles-Edmond, SIARRY Patrick
Graph Partitioning

BOULANGER Jean-Louis
Static Analysis of Software: The Abstract Interpretation

CAFERRA Ricardo
Logic for Computer Science and Artificial Intelligence

HOMES Bernard
Fundamentals of Software Testing

KORDON Fabrice, HADDAD Serge, PAUTET Laurent, PETRUCCI Laure
Distributed Systems: Design and Algorithms

KORDON Fabrice, HADDAD Serge, PAUTET Laurent, PETRUCCI Laure
Models and Analysis in Distributed Systems

LORCA Xavier
Tree-based Graph Partitioning Constraint

TRUCHET Charlotte, ASSAYAG Gerard
Constraint Programming in Music

VICAT-BLANC PRIMET Pascale *et al.*
Computing Networks: From Cluster to Cloud Computing

2010

AUDIBERT Pierre
Mathematics for Informatics and Computer Science

BABAU Jean-Philippe *et al.*
Model Driven Engineering for Distributed Real-Time Embedded Systems

BOULANGER Jean-Louis
Safety of Computer Architectures

MONMARCHE Nicolas *et al.*
Artificial Ants

PANETTO Hervé, BOUDJLIDA Nacer
Interoperability for Enterprise Software and Applications 2010

SIGAUD Olivier *et al.*
Markov Decision Processes in Artificial Intelligence

SOLNON Christine
Ant Colony Optimization and Constraint Programming

AUBRUN Christophe, SIMON Daniel, SONG Ye-Qiong *et al.*
Co-design Approaches for Dependable Networked Control Systems

2009

FOURNIER Jean-Claude
Graph Theory and Applications

GUEDON Jeanpierre
The Mojette Transform / Theory and Applications

JARD Claude, ROUX Olivier
Communicating Embedded Systems / Software and Design

LECOUTRE Christophe
Constraint Networks / Targeting Simplicity for Techniques and Algorithms

2008

BANÂTRE Michel, MARRÓN Pedro José, OLLERO Hannibal, WOLITZ Adam
Cooperating Embedded Systems and Wireless Sensor Networks

MERZ Stephan, NAVET Nicolas
Modeling and Verification of Real-time Systems

PASCHOS Vangelis Th
Combinatorial Optimization and Theoretical Computer Science: Interfaces and Perspectives

WALDNER Jean-Baptiste
Nanocomputers and Swarm Intelligence

2007

BENHAMOU Frédéric, JUSSIEN Narendra, O'SULLIVAN Barry
Trends in Constraint Programming

JUSSIEN Narendra
A TO Z OF SUDOKU

2006

BABAU Jean-Philippe *et al.*
From MDD Concepts to Experiments and Illustrations – DRES 2006

HABRIAS Henri, FRAPPIER Marc
Software Specification Methods

MURAT Cecile, PASCHOS Vangelis Th
Probabilistic Combinatorial Optimization on Graphs

PANETTO Hervé, BOUDJLIDA Nacer
Interoperability for Enterprise Software and Applications 2006 / IFAC-IFIP I-ESA'2006

2005

GÉRARD Sébastien *et al.*
Model Driven Engineering for Distributed Real Time Embedded Systems

PANETTO Hervé
Interoperability of Enterprise Software and Applications 2005